great hostels USA

An Inside Look at America's
Best Adventure Travel Accommodations

beaches | national parks | cities

Colleen Norwine

East Lansing, Michigan
USA

Great Hostels USA

Published by Sedobe Travel Guides,
an imprint of Sedobe, LLC

10 9 8 7 6 5 4 3 2

Visit us at www.greathostelsusa.com

Additionally, readers are encouraged to call hostels to confirm current information and prices. Feedback and updates are welcomed. Please send them to: info@greathostelsusa.com.

Cover design by AOR, Inc.
Interior design by Folio Bookworks
Editing by Maureen Haggerty

Library of Congress Control Number: 2005903683

ISBN-10: 0-9759807-0-X
ISBN-13: 978-0-9759807-0-5

Printed in Korea

Dedication

This book is dedicated to my three nephews, Brandon, Jake and Noah. I love you and I love watching your lives unfold before my eyes. As you grow into young men, remember that a winding road makes for an interesting journey. Don't be afraid to get off the highway if a back road's calling your name.

Acknowledgements

For their technical prowess, I owe a huge debt to Joan Wood and Beth Wampler at AOR, Inc. for the design of the book jacket, Liz Tufte at Folio Bookworks for the interior design and typesetting, and Maureen Haggerty for editing. Thanks for hanging in there on this labor of love.

The folks at Hostelling International were helpful and encouraging throughout the long and sometimes arduous writing process.

Heartfelt thanks go out to all the people who befriended me throughout my travels. Hostel owners, managers, workers and (especially) my fellow travelers. Your kindness will be forever remembered.

To my friends and colleagues at Ford Motor Company, Michigan State University, All Saints Episcopal Church and everyone at the Book Passage Travel Writers Conference, you taught and inspired me more than you'll ever know.

A big hug is in order for my family and friends whose love and support gave me the courage to trade my life of comfort and security for a life of never-ending joy and wonderment. I'm especially thankful for the strong women who've been friends and role models throughout the years: Noelle, Naghmana, Janice, Chris, Dawn, Barb, Tina, Kristi, Mona Leigh, Jan, Pam, Cyndi and, of course, Henrietta.

And, finally, my deepest gratitude is reserved for my mother, Lottie Norwine. Any success this book achieves is due to your unwavering emotional support, patient companionship on the road and tireless work as de facto accountant and fact checker. Without you, this book would simply not exist. And neither would I, come to think of it. Thanks, Mom.

Contents

Preface

What you hold in your hands is a byproduct of my love of travel and my belief in the personal and societal benefits that come of it. I make no claim to being an expert writer. My passion lies not in putting pen to paper, but in sharing information that can help people explore new territories and broaden their horizons.

Not long ago, I was working at one of the largest companies in the world. I had a good job. I was working with nice people, making plenty of money, progressing nicely in a career for which I had trained. But I kept having the same thoughts:

"My life is OK. Not bad. Just, well, *boring.* Actually, it's a *fine* life. I just don't think it's what I'm supposed to be doing. Ten years ago, I chose a path and it's served me well. I learned a lot, made a lot of friends and had some really interesting times. It was a great 10 years. But, 10 years is enough. It's time to do something else. I don't know what it will be – but it will be *something else.*"

More or less, that was the monologue. In my head. Every day. For over a year.

Some people subsequently called it a *midlife crisis,* but that term really didn't fit. I was neither old enough to be midway through my life nor unhappy enough to be in crisis. It was more like a *third-of-the-way-through funk.*

Whatever it was, it was enough to keep me talking to myself. And listening to what my subconscious was saying.

"What do I really want to do? What's my idea of fun these days? I'm single. I don't have to worry about anyone else. I can do whatever I want. Am I really ready to chuck it all? Ready to trade my safe, comfortable, predictable life and career for a leap into the unknown – all because of a gut feeling that there's something more out there for me?"

Pretty heady questions. The funny thing is, they weren't really tough to answer once I got around to asking them. Basically, it was the proverbial case of *if not now, when*?

And so I was off. I planned to spend a year traveling across the United States. In the course of one long road trip, I'd visit all the places I'd ever wanted to see in my home country – and maybe find an amazing new place to live. Ten years of the Midwest was plenty, I'd decided. I wasn't sure of my next destination, but I figured I'd know it when I arrived. (Actually, I was secretly hoping it would be overwhelmingly obvious. The heavens would open up while birds sang . . . that sort of thing.)

I said goodbye to everyone at the company, stored my stuff at a friend's place and packed my car. I was set. My plan was sketchy, but workable. I'd drive in a big U – heading south from Seattle down to San Diego, east to Florida and north up the coast all the way to Nova Scotia. My route was to be a rambling one, zigzagging between the coast and the mountains, taking note of everything in between.

The only thing I lacked was a trusty guidebook to help me find good hostels along my route. From the onset, I knew that I'd be hostelling my way across the country. I'd frequently stayed in hostels on weekend vacations and I loved the opportunity they provided to step into a completely different way of life: open, genuine and adventurous. Hostels attract the coolest people! I'd encountered many hostellers on 'round-the-world trips and always felt inspired by the tales they told. I knew hostels had the sort of atmosphere where I'd find support and enthusiasm for my own personal adventure.

I also knew from experience, however, that there are good hostels and there are bad hostels. And I intended to avoid the bad ones at all costs. I wanted the camaraderie and the inexpensive price tags that characterize hostelling. But I expected clean, attractive accommodations in safe neighborhoods. A hostel guidebook seemed the obvious answer. (I like hostel websites, but prefer to use them as supplements to a book I can pull out of my pack whenever the mood strikes me.) To cut a long story short, I never found the book I was looking for. So I decided to write it myself.

This is that book, and I hope it serves you well. I wrote it with a few key principles in mind. First, I included only hostels I could personally recommend. Extra weight is a backpacker's enemy, and I can see no sense in carrying around 100 extra pages describing hostels that don't measure up. Second, I based the reviews on my own overnight stays. Third, I accepted no money or favors in exchange for positive reviews or inclusion in the book. The only advertisement is one for Hostelling International, a nonprofit organization dedicated to promoting hostel travel. I included it because I'm a big supporter of the organization's mission, but I advised HI that my support for its work would not influence my assessment of individual HI facilities. And it didn't. Many HI hostels earned a place in the book, but some did not. The organization respected my principles and never tried to influence my evaluations.

I've created the best hostel guide I could, in an effort to encourage more people to experience hostelling. Hostels are one of the coolest ways to travel, especially if you're making your way on your own. Armed with this guide, you shouldn't care if your friends don't have the time or money to accompany you. Leave them at home. And leave everything else behind, too – your worries, your responsibilities, everyone's preconceived notions about and expectations of you – everything that leads to a closed mind and small world. Escape from it all and embark on new experiences. Meet new friends and see the world through their eyes. Hop in the car or board the train and just *go*. Explore all that America has to offer – eating, dancing and museum-hopping in the cities and hiking, biking and swimming in the mountains and oceans. But, even more importantly, meeting people who are not a bit like you or the friends who are checking the mail for the postcards you promised to send. Share meals with your new friends. Swap stories. Create new memories and learn from each other. Be prepared, though. You're likely to learn a lot about yourself along the way.

In the end, that's what my year of hostelling was all about. It was an unforgettable experience. I wish the same for you, and I hope this guide helps you make it happen.

See. Do. Be.
Colleen

Hostelling 101

What Is a Hostel?

To the best of my knowledge, a German schoolteacher introduced the concept of hostelling in 1907. During the summers and weekends, he transformed rural schoolhouses into inexpensive accommodations for students. His goal was to encourage more young people to travel, and he concentrated on bringing city kids to the country. The hostelling movement expanded to other countries after World War I and the first hostel in the United States opened in 1934. Hostelling has changed a lot over the past century. Age restrictions have been eliminated and other rules and regulations have been relaxed. What *hasn't* changed is hostelling's goal of encouraging people to travel, explore and learn.

You'll find that some modern-day hostels operate independently. Others belong to a hostel network. The largest nonprofit hostel organization in the world, Hostelling International (HI) operates over 100 hostels in the United States. Many of them are featured in this book. A $25 annual membership gives HI members a $3/night discount at most HI hostels. Independent hostels are run by owners who choose to operate without belonging to a network. Both types of hostels can be wonderful. In conducting research for this book, I applied the same criteria when evaluating HI facilities and independent hostels and found favorites in both categories.

Every hostel has its own personality. A hostel can be a 12-story high-rise building, a Victorian home or a lighthouse. But, universally, the biggest difference you'll find is between urban hostels and those in smaller towns. Hostels located in small towns or near national parks or seashores tend to be smaller, more personal, and rich in atmosphere and character. Big city hostels are more institutional in nature but provide outstanding value and a host of such useful amenities as a concierge desk or free neighborhood walking tours.

While each hostel is unique, all hostels have "common areas" and dorm rooms. These communal areas are what make a hostel a hostel.

Common Areas

Every hostel has rooms or gathering spaces that are shared by all guests and designed primarily to help guests meet and interact. For 90% of hostels, this includes a kitchen, dining area and living room/den, which is usually referred to as the "common room."

Hostel kitchens are high-traffic areas and they're especially important for long-distance travelers. Eating out gets old after a while. And expensive. When you're far from home, a chance to prepare your favorite foods can be a welcome change from restaurant fare. Most hostel kitchens are equipped with a refrigerator, stove, oven, and full assortment of dishes, pots, pans and utensils. Guests may store food on designated shelves and in the refrigerator and are asked to write their names on food and groceries not meant to be shared by all. Many hostel refrigerators feature a communal section for basics, like butter and ketchup, donated by guests who are heading home. There is no charge to use anything in the kitchen. But you will be expected to wash your own dishes and clean the cooking area you use.

The rest of the common rooms are less uniform, and their size and furnishings depend on the nature of the hostel. Big city hostels generally have large rooms with long tables and chairs, reminiscent of school cafeterias. Smaller hostels have cozier rooms that vary from contemporary living and dining rooms to dens with dated plaid couches. Almost every hostel has a small library of books and provides Internet access. But only about half have televisions. In a few hostels, the common area may simply be a front porch or courtyard with picnic tables.

Common area – large, city hostel

Common area – smaller hostel

Dining area

Kitchen

Dorm Rooms

While most hostels have at least one private room, 95% of guests stay in the dorms. Since many hostellers require low-cost sleeping accommodations – especially those on trips lasting several months – a facility had to have at least one dorm room in order to be classified as a hostel for this book.

Dorms are furnished with single beds, usually in the form of bunk beds. Rooms range in size and may sleep as few as four or as many as 24 guests. Smaller rooms are generally preferable; fewer roommates mean less clutter and nighttime noise. These are community rooms, so you will usually be sharing a room with people you didn't know before you arrived. It isn't as weird as it sounds though, so long as you're the social type. Spending the night in a hostel dorm is basically like summer camp for adults.

Dorm beds are rarely made up when you arrive. Upon check-in, complimentary or rented sheets are given to guests who haven't brought their own. (No sleeping bags allowed.) It's customary to make your bed as soon as you arrive. Smart, too. Making a bed marks the bed as *yours* and no one is allowed to move your stuff to another bed.

Most dorm rooms are pretty basic, furnished with little more than bunk beds and lockers. You will find that they vary quite a bit in size, though. Some have few beds (see below, left picture); others sleep up to 24 guests (see below, right picture).

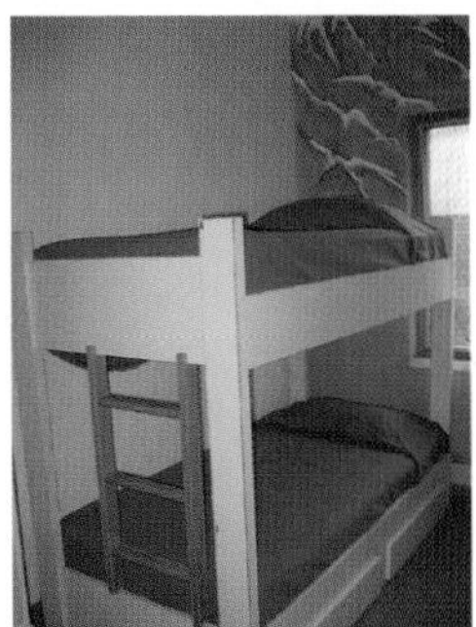

Small dorm room

Large dorm room

Why Go Hostelling?

Hostels are different for every visitor.

At the very least, a hostel is an inexpensive place to sleep. A bed in a dorm room costs about $19 a night and two people can split a private room for about $45. You'll be hard-pressed to find a better deal than that. And for many people, the low cost is a good enough reason to stay in a hostel.

Done right, however, hostelling can be a lot more than sleeping on the cheap. It can be an adventure, an escape from the routine of everyday life. It's an opportunity to meet and hang out with people from all over the world. Sixty percent of guests in U.S. hostels are visiting from other countries. Introduce yourself to other guests when you check in and you'll soon be swapping life stories and travel tales with people from all over the world.

Traveling solo? No problem. Most hostel guests are unaccompanied travelers looking to make new friends. At hostels, it's easy to form an impromptu tour group. Just let your roommates know what's on your agenda – trail hike, sightseeing or pub crawl – and invite people to join you. You're bound to have at least one taker. Hostels are transient by nature. Everyone is just stopping in for a brief visit before moving on to a new destination or returning home to resume "real life." The transient nature of things means that friendships are formed quickly and things that matter back home don't matter here at all. People will ask where you've come from and where you're headed, but no one cares where you work or how much money you make. It's an uncomplicated environment that fosters authentic, easy friendships.

Common Hostel Misconceptions

1. **Hostels are dirty, scary places.**

   Well, some hostels *are* dirty and scary. But others are great places. The purpose of this book is to help you avoid the first and discover the second. I visited over 200 hostels, but recommend and profile only 97 in this book. If you stick to the places I've included, you can travel with confidence.

2. **Hostels don't exist in the United States.**

   Hostels originated in Europe and have flourished in Australia/New Zealand, so those tend to be the locations most people associate with hostelling. But hostels are also thriving in the United States: I visited hundreds of hostels in the course of researching this book and I didn't get to them all. There are many others I was unable to visit. A few hostels do close from time to time. However, it seems that for every one that closes, a new one opens.

3. **Hostels are only for students and other "young" people.**

   This is in an outdated misconception about hostelling. The European hostel network was created for young student travelers. Originally called "youth hostels," the first facilities welcomed only guests under the age of 25. As Hostelling International (HI) grew to become the world's largest hostel network, with branches in almost every country, hostelling outgrew the old boundaries and restrictions. The U.S. branch of HI has eliminated upper age restrictions in all its facilities. This tendency to deemphasize youth isn't limited to HI hostels. Some independent or network-affiliated hostels have minimum age limits – especially for those not traveling with parents or chaperones. But not one of the hostels I visited while researching this book had an upper age limit for guests.

4. **Hostels are only for international travelers.**

   Hostel guests in the United States include a mix of domestic and international travelers. Forty percent are Americans and 60% come from other countries. Most international hostellers who visit the United States come from Western Europe, the United Kingdom and Australia/New Zealand. Important, but smaller, contingents of visitors hail from Asia, Eastern Europe, and Latin America. While a handful of urban hostels restrict admittance to travelers from other countries, 98% welcome both international and domestic travelers. This diversity incomparably enriches the hostel experience. Hostellers are always ready to share their stories and unique perspectives. International hostellers learn about America by living with Americans and local residents enjoy the most international experience possible without leaving the United States.

5. **Membership is required to stay in a hostel.**

   No hostel in the United States requires guests to be members of any organization. However, hostels that are members of a national or international organization typically offer discounted rates to members. Membership can be purchased at the front desk of many hostels and is a good investment for a traveler who plans to visit more than four hostels in one year. (Note: A membership is required to stay in the dorms of a few HI facilities during the busy summer months. Where that's the case, I've noted it in the hostel profile.)

6. **Hostel guests must do chores.**

   This is no longer the case. In days past, each guest was required to perform one small chore – such as sweeping the kitchen – each morning. This method of minimizing cleaning costs and keeping hostel rates low wasn't a bad idea, but 21st-century guests never warmed to the concept. So while some hostels make it clear that they'd be thrilled if you helped out, it's strictly on a volunteer basis.

Helpful Hints for Hostel Travel

1. **Call ahead.** Nothing is worse than showing up and finding out there's no room at the inn. Reservations are especially important during the summer. You'll also want to verify check-in times, since many hostels are closed during portions of the day.

2. **Dress the part.** Hostels are casual. Shorts, jeans and flip-flops are the norm unless you're a business traveler staying in a big city hostel. Think *explorer,* rather than *tourist.* One caveat: Older men need to walk a fine line. *Casual* is good. Looking like you're a scary homeless person is bad.

3. **Pack smart.** Bring a lock for the lockers, earplugs for the dorms and a flashlight so you won't disturb others when you make midnight bathroom runs. Bathroom items aren't provided, so you'll need to bring your own towel, soap and toiletries. If the hostel requires you to produce a passport, don't leave home without yours. Packing one paperback book is a good idea. When you're finished reading it, you'll find many hostels allow you to trade your book for one in their library. A driver whose car isn't crammed may want to pack laundry detergent, a cooler of food and a set of sheets. Sleeping on your own sheets helps provide a home-away-from-home feel and makes it unnecessary to rent linens from the hostel. Last but not least, be sure to take along a journal so you can record your experiences and impressions.

4. **Follow hostel protocol.** The first thing you do when you check in is make up a bed to mark it as yours. Then neatly store your stuff. Use a locker if one is available. Store items next to, or under, your bed otherwise. For the rest of your stay, the rules are easy: Clean up your cooking area and wash your dishes if you use the kitchen. Don't bring in alcohol if it is not allowed. Be quiet and don't wake your roommates if you come in late. And don't leave your personal items in the bathroom. When it's time for you to go home, clean up after yourself. Strip your bed and leave the sheets in the designated spot.

5. **Participate.** If you just want to commune with nature, a quiet hostel will suit you fine. Most travelers who choose to hostel are sociable by nature, though, and will appreciate that most facilities offer ample opportunities for guests to meet and mingle. Free walking tours are great ways to make new friends. Or just strike up a conversation with guests hanging out in the common room. Offering extra spaghetti, popcorn and other free food also works wonders.

6. **Plan for lock-outs.** Many hostels are closed for portions of the day and guests aren't allowed to stay in the building during those hours. Hostellers travel to experience their surroundings – not to sit inside all day – so being locked out isn't a big deal. But it helps to plan ahead to minimize any inconvenience. Outfit your backpack with maps, a water bottle and other essentials when you head out for the afternoon.

7. **Be generous.** If you have extra food, offer it to someone else. If you're driving into town, at least consider giving someone a ride. (But don't chauffeur anyone who seems weird or scary.)

8. **Don't be naïve.** Hostellers are a reflection of society: Most are honest, but a few can't be trusted. Be generous of spirit, but don't allow yourself to be vulnerable. Leave valuable jewelry and irreplaceable items at home. Use lockers whenever they're available. Don't loan money. And trust your instincts – especially when it comes to intimate encounters. Many a romance has blossomed between hostellers, so be open to that possibility. But if something just doesn't feel right, don't give the other person the benefit of the doubt. Don't even think twice about it. Go meet someone new.

9. **Listen more than you talk.** Hostelling is a great opportunity to broaden your horizons and expose yourself to other points of view. Travelers from all across the globe can introduce you to a variety of worldviews. Be sure to share your insights, but take in other perspectives before you do. You might discover a new way of looking at things.

10. **Ask hostel staff and fellow hostellers for recommendations.** Staff members know which sights are worth visiting and which restaurants are in your price range. Yesterday's hot nightspot may be old news today, but the locals can generally point you in the right direction. And their advice will be more current than recommendations you'll find in any book (including this one!) Ask fellow guests about hostels you plan to visit. They can tell you about landmarks that point the way to a hard-to-find destination. If there's a cool pub or a spectacular hiking trail nearby, they'll know about it. In short, the best way to decide which sights you must see and which experiences you'd rather avoid is to listen to someone who's been there and done that.

Hostel Review Explanations & Definitions

Hostel reviews include the following information:

HOSTEL NAME
Address
Phone number
Fax number
E-mail address
Website

~ what to expect ~

This is where you can read about what you'll find when you get to the hostel. Each review is different, customized to provide the most useful information about that particular facility and location. In general, however, you'll learn what types of sleeping accommodations are available, the condition and décor of the facility, the types of people and atmosphere you're likely to encounter (lively or mellow) and some things to do in the area.

I've included multiple pictures in each review because, as they say, a picture's worth a thousand words. A peek inside the hostel will give you the best sense of what it's like. The pictures were taken by an enthusiastic but truly amateur photographer – me. You're likely to find fancier pictures of each facility on its website. My goal wasn't to show you what the hostel looks like on its best day, but rather what it looks like on an average day. I've provided a look at both the exterior and interior of the hostel. One interior shot is usually of the common area, since that's where you'll spend the most time. If space allows, an additional shot highlights either a private bedroom or some other room/space unique to the facility. I rarely include pictures of dorm rooms because if you've seen one, you've more or less seen them all. If a dorm is unique, I'll show you. Absent evidence to the contrary, it's probably a simple room furnished with little more than bunk beds and lockers. Read "what is a hostel" to find out more about dorm rooms.

~ fast facts ~

Dorm Rates: price for one bed in a dorm room

Private Rooms: price for a private room; generally the same price for either 1 or 2 guests

Credit Cards: credit cards accepted for payment, if any; "AMEX" is used as an abbreviation for American Express

Network: inclusion in any hostel network (e.g., Hostelling International, Hostels USA, etc.)

Beds: either "spring mattresses" (like your bed at home) or "foam mattresses" (thin mattresses often used with cots)

Kitchen: availability (yes/no) and key features/limitations (e.g., handicapped-accessible or outside location)

Bathrooms: either "house-style" (holds one person like your bathroom at home) or dorm-style (accommodates several people at once); either "private" (attached to bedroom) or "shared" (located down the hall)

Lockers: availability (yes/no) and other key aspects (such as location, number or size)

Extras: hostel amenities

Be Aware: things that might be of concern to some regarding the neighborhood or hostel

In the Area: local attractions

Local Tip: insider information obtained from locals

Closest Free Internet: free Internet station closest to the hostel

Parking: availability and rates for parking and shuttles

Season: time of year/seasons the hostel is open

Office Hours: times you can expect to reach someone on the phone or find someone at the front desk

Lock-out: time of day when the hostel is closed and guests are expected to amuse themselves elsewhere

Size: number of beds in the hostel

is this hostel great for you?

Every hostel in the book is a great hostel for someone – but not necessarily for everyone. This section provides a quick assessment of whether each location is especially suited for different types of hostellers: solo women, party animals, over age 30, over age 50, couples, families and groups.

I've obviously had to impose several stereotypes in order to develop these little summaries. So take these comments with a grain of salt. If you're 39 years old and looking for a wild good time, the "party animal" comments may be more relevant for you than the "over 30" observations. If you're a physically fit 60-year-old who enjoys hanging out with people of all ages but are concerned about safety, the "solo women" summary might be most useful for you. Read over the entries, get a feel for how they mesh with your personal style and use them as tools to help you create the traveling adventure that's right for you.

SOLO WOMEN: *safe hostel and neighborhood? easy to make friends? peaceful getaway spot?*

PARTY ANIMALS: *lively crowd? alcohol allowed onsite? bars nearby? curfew?*

OVER 30: *private rooms available? cultural attractions nearby?*

OVER 50: *mixed-age crowd? mobility concerns? rooms conducive to a good night's sleep (number of guests in dorms, spring vs. foam mattresses, etc.)?*

COUPLES: *double beds in private rooms? romantic atmosphere?*

FAMILIES: *mellow, family-friendly crowd? kid attractions onsite or nearby?*

GROUPS: *large enough? big kitchen and dining area? meeting rooms available?*

U.S. Hostels

Arizona Hostels

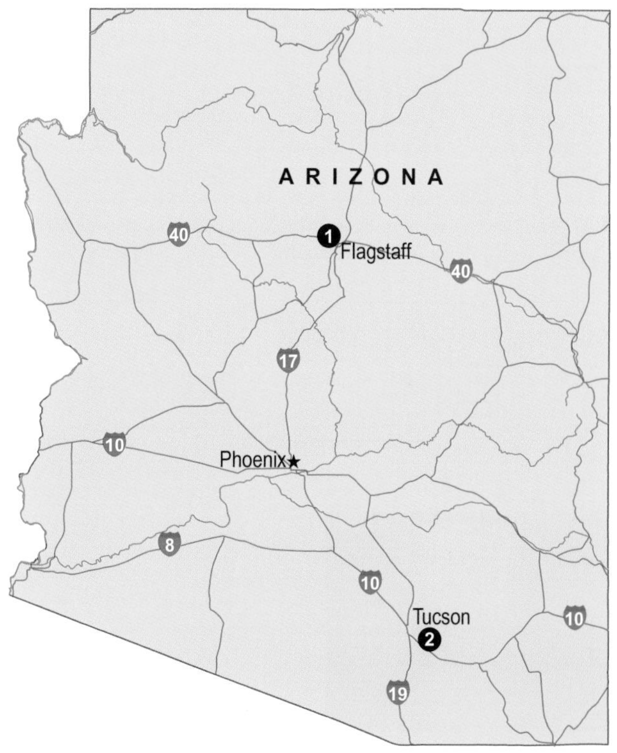

1 Flagstaff
Grand Canyon International Hostel

2 Tucson
Hotel Congress

Flagstaff, Arizona

GRAND CANYON INTERNATIONAL HOSTEL
19 S. San Francisco
Flagstaff, AZ 86001
Phone: (928) 779-9421 or (888) 442-2692
Fax: n/a
E-mail: info@grandcanyonhostel.com
Website: www.grandcanyonhostel.com

~ what to expect ~

I came for a night and stayed for four. I love this hostel! Staying here is like bunking at a friend's place – because the guests are quickly enveloped in one another's lives.

Flagstaff is the big town nearest the Grand Canyon. Young and old, solo travelers and couples, international travelers and Americans, all come to visit the Canyon and they all bring their stories with them. Breakfast may be enlivened with tales of one adventurer's first road trip or another's 40th birthday celebration.

Travelers without cars will be happy to know that a van tour company operates out of the hostel. Daily trips to the Grand Canyon alternate with visits to Sedona, a nearby artists community.

A two-story refurbished house with hardwood floors, the hostel can accommodate 30 guests in dorm rooms and seven private rooms with queen-size beds. Three of the dorm rooms have just three beds – one set of bunks and a twin bed – and can also be used as private rooms. All guests share the four bathrooms along the hall.

The dorm rooms are decorated with homey curtains and comforters. Furnished with only two sets of bunks, the small but cozy rooms can be a pleasant change for travelers accustomed to dorms that sleep 10 or 12 people. In-room sinks and refrigerators round out the amenities.

There's a kitchen upstairs and another downstairs. Each morning, a free breakfast of oatmeal, toast, coffee and fresh fruit is served in a spacious first-floor dining room. Evenings often find guests sprawled on the couch in the TV room or surfing the Web in the office. Guests are also permitted to visit the owner's other hostel, The DuBeau Hostel. Located just a few blocks away, the DuBeau isn't as homey as the Grand Canyon International. But it does boast a pool table and a nice fireplace.

~ fast facts ~

Dorm Rates: $14–16, vary by season

Private Rooms: $30–37, vary by season

Credit Cards: MasterCard & Visa

Network: n/a

Beds: spring mattresses

Kitchen: yes – 2

Bathrooms: shared, dorm-style

Lockers: no

Extras: free breakfast, VCR movies, laundry, high-speed Internet access, phone cards, van tours to Sedona ($25) and the Grand Canyon ($50)

Season: all year

Office Hours: 7am–midnight

Lock-out: n/a

Size: 30 dorm beds & 7 private rooms

Be Aware: College-housing neighborhood is nothing fancy.

In The Area: Grand Canyon, Sedona artists community.

Local Tip: Great food at the Italian restaurant/deli across the street. Featuring a fireplace in the coffee shop, the town's huge Barnes & Noble bookstore is a welcoming foul-weather refuge.

Closest Free Internet: public library

Parking: free off-street parking; free pick-up at the bus station

is this hostel great for you?

SOLO WOMEN Yes. Like staying at a friend's house.

PARTY ANIMALS No. The sister hostel a few blocks away, the DuBeau Hostel, is a better bet.

OVER 30 Yes. Nice, comfortable camaraderie. Guests at this hostel range from 22–64 years.

OVER 50 Yes. Check out the Chapel of the Holy Cross in Sedona.

COUPLES Yes. Several nice private rooms are available.

FAMILIES Yes, if everyone's a hiker.

GROUPS No. Not big enough to accommodate most groups.

Tucson, Arizona

HOTEL CONGRESS
311 East Congress St.
Tucson, AZ 85701
Phone: (520) 622-8848 or
(800) 722-8848
Fax: (520) 792-6366
E-mail: hotel@hotelcongress.com
Website: www.hotelcongress.com

~ what to expect ~

You'll love this place. Or hate it. I had a ball. My friend won't ever go back.

Our intense reactions stem from the dance club on the floor below the hostel. Techno music flows through the speakers and reverberates up through the floorboards. Those who join in and let their hair down will have fun. Those who'd prefer an early night won't be happy campers.

The hotel, hostel, club and dining establishments are housed in a multi-story historic building in old downtown Tucson. The first floor is very modern, but the rooms upstairs are more in keeping with the historic building.

In addition to the dance club, the first floor of the building houses a café and restaurant which hostellers share with the public. There aren't many common areas upstairs. A small TV room is furnished with a single couch, a couple of chairs and a computer with Internet access. Hotel Congress has no kitchen or dining room.

Although this is primarily a hotel, four low-frills hostel rooms are available. Each room is furnished with a dresser, radio and sink. Two of the rooms have bunk beds; the other two rooms have twin beds. One room sleeps four people. Each of the other rooms sleeps two. These small rooms provide more privacy than typically found in a hostel.

~ fast facts ~

Dorm Rates:	$20–25	**Season:**	all year
Private Rooms:	$49–59 (1), $59–69 (2), $79–99 (3–4)	**Office Hours:**	24 hours
		Lock-out:	n/a
		Size:	4 hostel rooms w/2 beds apiece
Credit Cards:	MasterCard, Visa, Discover, AMEX		
Network:	n/a		
Beds:	spring mattresses		
Kitchen:	no		
Bathrooms:	shared, dorm-style		
Lockers:	no		
Extras:	free linens & towels, onsite dance club, onsite café, elegant banquet room for 150, TV, free high-speed Internet access		
Be Aware:	The dance club music will keep you up past midnight; hostel membership required for dorms.		
In The Area:	Biosphere, Saguaro National Park		
Local Tip:	dance club downstairs.		
Closest Free Internet:	onsite		
Parking:	free onsite parking; near bus station		

is this hostel great for you?

SOLO WOMEN Yes, especially if you're lookin' to hook up.

PARTY ANIMALS Yes, dance club downstairs.

OVER 30 Only if you're an over-30 party animal.

OVER 50 No. You'll not get a good night's sleep here.

COUPLES Maybe. A fun place, but not a romantic place.

FAMILIES No. No. No.

GROUPS Maybe. See the above comments.

California Hostels

1. **Cambria**
   Bridge Street Inn
2. **Klamath**
   HI – Redwood National Park
3. **Los Altos**
   HI – Hidden Villa
4. **Los Angeles / Fullerton**
   HI – L.A. / Fullerton
5. **Los Angeles / Santa Monica**
   HI – L.A. / Santa Monica
6. **Los Angeles / Venice Beach**
   Cadillac Hotel
7. **Mammoth Lakes**
   Davison Street Guesthouse
8. **Midpines**
   HI – Midpines (Yosemite Bug Hostel)
9. **Montara**
   HI – Point Montara Lighthouse
10. **Monterey**
    HI – Monterey (Carpenters Hall)
11. **Pescadero**
    HI – Pigeon Point Lighthouse
12. **Sacramento**
    HI – Sacramento (The Mansion)
13. **San Diego**
    Ocean Beach International Hostel
14. **San Diego**
    HI – San Diego, Point Loma
15. **San Francisco**
    The Elements
16. **San Francisco**
    HI – Fisherman's Wharf
17. **San Francisco**
    HI – City Center
18. **San Luis Obispo**
    Hostel Obispo (HI – San Luis Obispo)
19. **Santa Barbara**
    Santa Barbara Tourist Hostel
20. **Santa Cruz**
    HI – Santa Cruz
21. **Saratoga**
    HI – Sanborn Park Hostel

Cambria, California

BRIDGE STREET INN
4314 Bridge St.
Cambria, CA 93428
Phone: (805) 927-7653
Fax: n/a
E-mail: BridgeStreetInn@yahoo.com
Website: www.bridgestreetinncambria.com

~ what to expect ~

This is a quiet, pretty little hostel in a quiet, pretty little town.

The B&B industry appears to be thriving in this peaceful, romantic setting. Visitors arrive each weekend to window-shop, enjoy fine food and stroll through the charming village hand in hand. One gets the feeling that the biggest conflict in town is over which resident has the greenest thumb. Everywhere you look, you'll see flower boxes overflowing with honeysuckle, lavender, geraniums and roses. The Bridge Street Inn is no exception.

The delights of Cambria and the Bridge Street Inn are among hostelling's best-kept secrets. The owner's decision to remain independent rather than affiliate with one of the hostel networks has undoubtedly helped preserve its relative anonymity.

One small room of the 15-room inn is reserved exclusively as a dorm for hostellers. Depending on who shows up in need of a bed, its three bunk beds may function as a coed dorm. Each bed is shielded by a curtain similar to those that afforded privacy to sleeping bunks on vintage railway cars. A room with one double bed and one set of bunks is situated behind the dorm. It can be used as either a dorm or a private room, as needs dictate. Most guests opt to stay in one of the three private second-floor rooms decorated with floral curtains and duvets. The "couples room" is furnished with one double bed. Each of the other two sleeps up to three guests. The dorm and private rooms share individual bathrooms located in the hall.

Downstairs walls are adorned with antique portraits of the owner's ancestors and a handmade quilt. A couch, dining room table, chairs and wood-burning stove create a somewhat rumpled but comfortable and relaxing living room–dining area.

A small kitchen is available for guest use and a free continental breakfast is provided each morning.

~ fast facts ~

Dorm Rates: $20

Private Rooms: $40–70

Credit Cards: MasterCard & Visa

Network: n/a

Beds: spring mattresses in privates; foam in dorms

Kitchen: yes

Bathrooms: private, house-style

Lockers: no

Extras: free coffee, tea & continental breakfast, free linens, rent the entire facility for $300-400

Season: all year

Office Hours: 5pm–9pm

Lock-out: 10:30am–5pm (Private rooms are accessible during the day.)

Size: 11 beds

Be Aware: Guests in one bedroom must walk through the dorm to get to their room. No Greyhound service north from here.

In The Area: Hearst Castle, shopping, beach, Paso Robles winetasting

Local Tip: Lunch at Robin's is a treat.

Closest Free Internet: n/a – fee service at town pharmacy and wireless Internet café

Parking: free parking at hostel

is this hostel great for you?

SOLO WOMEN Yes. Nice place to relax. But expect to encounter a lot of couples.

PARTY ANIMALS No. The hostel, and town, will be too quiet for you.

OVER 30 Yes. Good place to meet up with friends.

OVER 50 Yes. National Public Radio and breakfast teas set the tone here.

COUPLES Yes. Romance is in the air.

FAMILIES Yes, if the family is small and the children well-behaved.

GROUPS Yes, if you rent the entire inn. Too small otherwise.

Klamath, California

HI – REDWOOD NATIONAL PARK
14480 Highway 101
Klamath, CA 95548
Phone: (707) 482-8265
Fax: (707) 482-4665
E-mail: info@redwoodhostel.com
Website: www.norcalhostels.org

~ what to expect ~

The Redwood Hostel's convenient location makes it a must-stop for almost every hosteller touring the West Coast. Those traveling by car can reach either San Francisco or Portland in just one (long) day.

While location alone isn't a bad reason to spend a night here, it would be a shame not to allot some time to check out the "big trees" before rushing off to another destination.

Redwood Forest is home to trees that tower 300 feet above your head. The average tree is over 600 years old; some have been alive for over 2,000 years. While the trees are everywhere, the biggest are 15–20 miles from the hostel. A brief hike in the groves is enough to get a feel for their magnificence, but nature lovers will want to reserve at least a day to fully explore the park.

The hostel sits high on a hill and looks out over the beach across the street. In good weather, guests can open their bedroom windows and fall asleep to the sound of the waves. An environmentally themed décor brings the mood of the beach and forest inside. Redwood Forest posters hang all around the hostel.

Sleeping accommodations include one men's dorm, one women's dorm, one coed dorm and one private room. The dorms are fairly big and basic. The private room is a little nicer, decorated with coordinating curtains and rug. Everyone shares the same freshly painted bathrooms. The common rooms include a white tiled kitchen and a large living room with lots of windows and cushy sofas.

Every room in the hostel is spotless, thanks largely to the hostellers themselves. This is one of the few hostels that still asks guests to perform a daily chore. Early risers get to pick "wipe kitchen countertops," while the laggards will be asked to "clean a bathroom." While I don't mind doing my part, I made a special effort to be an early riser.

~ fast facts ~

Dorm Rates: $16–$20 (members & non-members)

Private Rooms: $45 for 1–2 people (2 rooms with queen-size beds)

Credit Cards: MasterCard, Visa, Discover & JCB

Network: HI

Beds: foam mattresses

Kitchen: yes

Bathrooms: shared, house-style

Lockers: no

Season: March–November

Office Hours: 8am–10am & 5pm–10pm

Lock-out: 10am–5pm

Size: 30 beds

Extras: Internet access, wood-burning stove, basic groceries sold at office, laundry

Be Aware: One dorm is coed. Small daily chores are requested (but not required) of guests. Nothing is located within walking distance: Bring groceries and try not to arrive during lock-out. There are several flights of stairs between the parking lot and the hostel.

In The Area: Redwood Forest State Park, hiking; jet-boat river excursions at Gold Beach, Oregon

Local Tip: Greyhound bus (flag) stop outside the hostel

Closest Free Internet: public library

Parking: free parking

is this hostel great for you?

SOLO WOMEN Yes. Hostel and area are very safe – the neighbors are trees.

PARTY ANIMALS No. You'll be bored.

OVER 30 Yes. While most guests are in their 20s, the rest range from 30s to 50s.

OVER 50 Yes, the forest drives/hikes are fun.

COUPLES Yes. A nice private room is available.

FAMILIES No. No family rooms are available.

GROUPS Yes. Large kitchen and dining areas.

Los Altos, California

HI – HIDDEN VILLA
26870 Moody Rd.
Los Altos Hills, CA 94022
Phone: (650) 949-8648
Fax: (650) 949-8606
E-mail: hostel@hiddenvilla.org
Website: www.hiddenvilla.org

~ what to expect ~

Hidden Villa, a 1,600-acre nonprofit organic farm and wilderness preserve, is home to the oldest existing hostel in the United States.

Established in 1937, the hostel currently participates in several community programs. Used as a camp during the summer, the hostel is only open to the public October–May. Well-suited for a summer camp, the facility is also good for groups or families open to "roughing it" a bit.

The bedrooms and bathrooms are all in separate wood cabins situated a short walk from the main building. Bedrooms are rustic in décor but include such nice touches as large in-room lockers and reading lights for the bottom bunks.

The main building houses a large modern living room, dining room, screened porch and professional kitchen. Up-to-date décor and furnishings are found throughout: nothing old or shabby here. But solo travelers who arrive on a quiet night will want to have a good book handy. Because the office is in a separate building, striking up a conversation with a staff member isn't an option to ward off loneliness.

Those who've been hostelling through California for a while will appreciate the absence of a daytime lock-out. Guests are welcome to relax to their heart's content and encouraged to explore the eight miles of hiking trails that surround the hostel. City kids will get a kick out of visiting the farm-raised cows, sheep, goats, chickens and pigs.

~ fast facts ~

Dorm Rates:	$19 HI members, $22 non-members	**Season:**	October–May
Private Rooms:	$37–51	**Office Hours:**	8am–12pm & 4pm–9:30pm
Credit Cards:	MasterCard & Visa	**Lock-out:**	n/a
Network:	HI	**Size:**	34 beds
Beds:	foam mattresses		
Kitchen:	yes		
Bathrooms:	dorm-style , in a separate building		
Lockers:	yes		
Extras:	free Internet, organic farm, piano, outdoor BBQ and fire pit		
Be Aware:	Hostel is closed June–September; bathrooms & bedrooms are located in separate cabins.		
Local Tip:	no daytime lock-out		
Closest Free Internet:	public library		
Parking:	free parking at hostel		

is this hostel great for you?

SOLO WOMEN Maybe. Very safe, but could be boring.

PARTY ANIMALS No.

OVER 30 Yes. Best for those into organic farming.

OVER 50 Yes. But be aware that a trip to the bathroom will require an outdoor stroll.

COUPLES Yes. Private cabins are available.

FAMILIES Yes. Family cabins are available. Kids will enjoy the farm.

GROUPS Yes. Youth groups often make use of the large common areas and kitchen.

Los Angeles/Fullerton, California

HI – L.A./FULLERTON
1700 North Harbor Blvd.
Fullerton, CA 92835
Phone: (714) 738-3721
Fax: (714) 738-0925
E-mail: hifull@aol.com
Website: www.hihostels.com

~ what to expect ~

This homey 20-room hostel can be a nice change from the big Los Angeles hostels. Here, people tend to hang out and visit with each other on the screened front porch or in the living room.

Downstairs are the living room, kitchen, men's dorm and bathroom. Archways frame each room's entrance and the light-filled kitchen is a pleasant place to prepare a meal. The living room is the nicest room of all. People lounge on contemporary furniture to watch television or enjoy fireside chats. A table and chairs are available for dining, but most people take their meals on the porch in California's predictably pleasant and mild summer weather.

The women's dorm, the coed dorm and the women's bathroom are located upstairs. The bedrooms and bathrooms are clean but simple and each bedroom features storage lockers. Unfortunately, the bedrooms also feature plastic-covered foam mattresses. They're hygienic, but they're also noisy and uncomfortable.

This is a good hostel, but you wouldn't want to make it your base for exploring Los Angeles. L.A. is a sprawling metropolis and this hostel is quite a distance from Santa Monica, Hollywood and Venice Beach. Stay at the Santa Monica hostel on the days you intend to visit those areas. Come here to take in Disneyland or indulge in some peace and quiet.

~ fast facts ~

Dorm Rates:	$15 HI members, $17 non-members	**Season:**	June–September
Private Rooms:	n/a	**Office Hours:**	8am– 1:30pm & 2:30pm–11pm
Credit Cards:	MasterCard & Visa	**Lock-out:**	11:30am–4pm
Network:	HI	**Size:**	20 beds
Beds:	foam mattresses		
Kitchen:	yes		
Bathrooms:	shared, dorm-style		
Lockers:	yes, large		
Extras:	TV, fireplace, board games, screened front porch		
Be Aware:	no Internet or public phone; mattresses with plastic covers		
In The Area:	Disneyland		
Local Tip:	outstanding golf practice facility next door with driving range and 18-hole putting course		
Closest Free Internet:	public library		
Parking:	free onsite parking		

is this hostel great for you?

SOLO WOMEN Yes, if visiting Disneyland. No real reason to stay here otherwise.

PARTY ANIMALS No. Far, far from L.A. nightlife.

OVER 30 Yes. A slower, more intimate alternative to big city hostels.

OVER 50 Yes. Senior golfers get discount prices at the practice facility next door.

COUPLES Yes, if you're up for the coed dorm.

FAMILIES No. No private rooms are available.

GROUPS Yes, if small.

Los Angeles/Santa Monica, California

HI – L.A./SANTA MONICA
1617 Santa Rosa St.
Santa Monica, CA 90401
Phone: (310) 393-9913
Fax: (310) 393-1769
E-mail: reserve@HILosAngeles.org
Website: www.hiusa.org

~ what to expect ~

Los Angeles is unlike any other city in the United States. If you plan to explore it on your own, you'll need a thoughtful plan of attack.

Driving from one side of the city to the other takes two hours. Even longer if you hit rush-hour traffic. The same trip, using public transportation, will be a day-long excursion on a series of buses. Plan accordingly.

One of the best things about this hostel is that it provides a great base from which to explore the city. Venice Beach, known as much for people-watching opportunities as for its ocean views, is only a short walk from the front door. (Some travelers prefer to stay in the heart of that neighborhood. However, most will find that the fortune-tellers, psychedelic T-shirt booths and incense stands exhaust their entertainment potential in short order.) Just three blocks from this hostel, the Santa Monica beach is an ideal place to enjoy sand, sun and surf. International travelers looking to make the most of their currencies' strong exchange rate will love the Third Street Promenade. One block north of the hostel, this outdoor pedestrians-only mall displays all the latest fashions. From jazz clubs to English pubs, a variety of bars also populates this strip.

With more than 200 guests, the hostel caters as well as can be expected to the needs of individual travelers. The building is too big to be charming or quaint, but it's clean and well-organized. And it provides such cool free perks as movies, walking tours of city neighborhoods and a Saturday night comedy show. The HI travel shop next door sells maps, guidebooks and Amtrak tickets.

Guests may select dorm accommodations or private rooms. Each uncluttered dorm has 4–10 beds. Men traveling alone are not assigned to any of the coed dorms. Each of the 11 private rooms features two twin beds or a double bed. (Double beds have more comfortable mattresses.) The décor resembles a small, inexpensive motel room. Nothing fancy, but nothing especially ugly. Everyone shares the large stall-shower bathrooms located down the hall.

Spacious common areas include a kitchen, dining area, sitting room with piano, library with wireless Internet access, outdoor courtyard and TV and movie rooms. Conversation is more likely to be found among the smokers in the outdoor courtyard, but you won't find a lot of people just hanging around the hostel. Everyone here is on the go.

~ fast facts ~

Dorm Rates: $14-16, varies by season

Private Rooms: $67 for 1–2 members, $72 for 1–2 non-members

Credit Cards: MasterCard & Visa

Network: HI

Beds: foam mattresses in dorms & on single beds in private rooms; spring mattresses on double beds in private rooms

Kitchen: yes

Bathrooms: shared, dorm-style

Lockers: yes

Extras: free movies, free walking tours, free poetry readings & comedy shows, TV, Internet access, piano, library, tours, laundry facilities, breakfast café, travel store

Be Aware: few dishes provided in the kitchen; bathroom could be cleaner

In The Area: beach, shopping, lots of entertainment

Local Tip: Travel center next door sells guidebooks, train tickets & maps; good coffee across the street.

Closest Free Internet: public library

Parking: garage parking across from hostel

Season: all year

Office Hours: 24 hours

Lock-out: n/a

Size: 228 beds

is this hostel great for you?

SOLO WOMEN Yes. Walking tours, movie nights, craft classes and discounted city tours provide multiple opportunities to meet fellow travelers.

PARTY ANIMALS Yes. Share a cab to visit Hollywood clubs.

OVER 30 Yes. Best dollar value in L.A.

OVER 50 Yes. The clientele is a mix of all ages. Elevators carry guests to upper floors.

COUPLES Yes. Eleven private rooms are available.

FAMILIES Yes. A small dorm (4-6 beds) can be used as a family room.

GROUPS Yes. Well-suited for groups: plenty of beds, a very large kitchen and 45-seat dining area.

Los Angeles / Venice Beach, California

CADILLAC HOTEL
8 Dudley Ave.
Venice, California 90291
Phone: (310) 399-8876
Fax: (310) 399-4536
E-mail: reservations@thecadillachotel.com
Website: www.thecadillachotel.com

~ what to expect ~

You needn't worry if you walk into the Cadillac Hotel with sand in your shoes. That's par for the course at this hostel close by Venice's beach and boardwalk.

A trip to the hostel basement will help you get in shape for the beach, too. That's where you'll find an impressive weight room featuring aerobic machines and a sauna.

At the time of my last visit, the big, high-ceilinged common room attached to the lobby was unfocused and sparsely furnished. Several couches and chairs were scattered randomly around the room. A pool table and jukebox occupied one corner; an Internet kiosk took up another. The owners had been thinking about redecorating the room, so its appearance may be different when you visit. With any luck, the lobby's cool luminescent gold walls and Art Deco-inspired fixtures will provide design cues for the remodel. But even if they don't, you'll still be able to view an amazing little piece of history. Interestingly enough, a genuine artifact – a piece of the Berlin Wall – is embedded amidst the random furnishings. There's no kitchen or dining room at the Cadillac.

Most bedrooms in the Cadillac are typical hotel rooms. There are no private rooms dedicated to hostellers, so travelers wanting to pay hostel prices will have to bunk in one of the dorm rooms.

Anyone wanting a break from predictable HI offerings will do well to check out the Cadillac. Price, proximity to the beach and free parking are good reasons why these accommodations are in great demand. But if you want to stay in this hostel, be prepared to produce a valid passport.

~ fast facts ~

Dorm Rates: $26 summer, $22 September–May

Private Rooms: n/a in hostel; hotel rooms available

Credit Cards: MasterCard & Visa

Network: n/a

Beds: spring mattresses

Kitchen: no

Bathrooms: shared

Lockers: no

Extras: free linens and towels, weight room, sauna, wireless Internet access, Internet kiosks, pool table, laundry, group rates available

Be Aware: valid passport required; coed dorms

In The Area: Venice Beach 1 block away, other L.A. attractions are nearby.

Local Tip: A piece of the Berlin Wall is on display in the lobby.

Closest Free Internet: Venice & Ocean Park public libraries

Parking: free parking nearby

Season: all year

Office Hours: 24 hours

Lock-out: n/a

Size: 18 beds plus hotel

is this hostel great for you?

SOLO WOMEN Maybe, if coed dorms are acceptable.

PARTY ANIMALS Yes. No rules about alcohol here.

OVER 30 Not especially. Santa Monica's a better bet.

OVER 50 No. Wrong vibes.

COUPLES Maybe. No private hostel rooms, but dorms are coed.

FAMILIES No. No family hostel rooms.

GROUPS No. Too few hostel rooms for a group.

Mammoth Lakes, California

DAVISON STREET GUESTHOUSE
19 Davison St.
Mammoth Lakes, CA 93546
Phone: (760) 924-2188;
(858) 755-8648 for advance reservations
Fax: n/a
E-mail: n/a
Website: www.mammoth-guest.com

~ what to expect ~

It's only a matter of time until the hostel community discovers all that this unique guesthouse has to offer.

The lack of buzz so far is probably due to Davison Street Guesthouse being a private hostel, rather than one affiliated with a network. That's a shame, because it's every bit as good as any HI hostel I've ever visited.

As with any hostel located in a ski town, the time of year you visit determines the kind of experience you'll have. When the temperature plummets, the town springs to life. The ski resorts open for the business of schussing and slaloming, the free buses make runs around town and up to the slopes and the hostel fills. The summer brings a quieter in-town experience. Most who visit during warmer weather use the hostel as a base camp for day hikes or as a place to stay before or after visiting Yosemite National Park. It's the only hostel on the eastern side of the park.

The Guesthouse is a wood A-frame in a residential neighborhood. Giant pine trees and a 4' bear carving flank the entrance. You'll find a lot to like inside, and the common room will probably be at the top of your list. A full wall of floor-to-ceiling windows frames a panoramic scene of mountains and forests. During my visit, guests gathered on couches around a wood-burning stove to drink in the spectacular views and tell tales of their travels, their lives at home and their plans for the future.

There isn't a separate dining room, but a table in the kitchen adjacent to the common room seats four. The bedrooms all reflect recent updates. The private rooms are as nice as any you'd find in any area condo. The décor is mountain cabin – comforters and lamps decorated with images of bears and pine trees and refinished wood beds, dressers and night-stands. Less-fancy dorm rooms sport similar comforters on comfortable wood bunks.

Winter offers charming accommodations convenient to the ski slopes. Summer offers a cozy mountain lodge experience less than two hours from Yosemite. Both seasons are great times to visit. But drop in soon, before the secret gets out.

~ fast facts ~

Dorm Rates: $22–30 summer; $33–39 winter

Private Rooms: $45–65 shared bath, $63–84 private bath (summer) $72–94 shared bath, $94–110 private bath (winter)

Season: all year

Office Hours: varied

Lock-out: n/a

Size: 22 beds

Credit Cards: no

Network: n/a

Beds: spring mattresses

Kitchen: yes

Bathrooms: shared, house-style

Lockers: no

Extras: TV, wood-burning stove, rent entire facility for $500 (summer)–$710 (winter)

Be Aware: No onsite Internet; stairs must be climbed. Groups often rent the hostel. Be sure to call ahead.

In The Area: skiing, snowshoeing, snowmobiling, dogsled rides, ice skating, gondola rides, horseback riding, fishing, mountain biking, hiking, Yosemite National Park, Devil's Postpile

Local Tip: a good place to stop after visiting Lake Tahoe or Las Vegas or before heading into Yosemite

Closest Free Internet: public library, 5 blocks away

Parking: free parking at hostel; shuttle to ski slopes in the winter

is this hostel great for you?

SOLO WOMEN Yes. Very safe, clean and cozy.

PARTY ANIMALS Maybe. The town hops during ski season but sleeps in the summer.

OVER 30 Yes. You'll wish you could buy this place. Guaranteed.

OVER 50 Maybe. Most will prefer the quiet summers to ski season activity.

COUPLES Yes. Great private rooms.

FAMILIES No. Kids would disrupt the mellow hostel vibe.

GROUPS Yes, if the group is small (e.g., track team).

Midpines, California

HI – MIDPINES
(YOSEMITE BUG HOSTEL)
6979 Highway 140, P.O. Box 81
Midpines, CA 95345
Phone: (209) 966-6666
Fax: (209) 966-6667
E-mail: bughost@yosemitebug.com
Website: www.yosemitebug.com

~ what to expect ~

Nestled in the woods 25 miles southwest of Yosemite National Park, The Yosemite Bug feels like an extension of the park itself.

The center of this complex is the Main Lodge, which houses the Bug Café, the front office and several private rooms with shared bath. Beyond the lodge are cabins, which contain more private rooms with shared or private baths, and the dorm rooms. It's reminiscent of an old-fashioned summer camp.

The dorms are basic and they can get crowded. They work best for those using the hostel as an alternative to camping. Your best bet is a private room, where quilts and antique furniture make for a rustic B&B atmosphere. The private rooms are also likely to provide a better night's sleep. That's because the single and double beds are outfitted with spring mattresses instead of the standard foam dorm mattresses.

At the Bug, only the dorms are officially considered "the hostel." That means only that the no-alcohol HI policy doesn't apply to the rest of the facility. It's a small luxury to have a beer with dinner, but much appreciated after a day spent hiking or climbing. Few hostellers use the small, basic kitchen. Most guests – as well as quite a few local residents – buy their evening meal from the café. A $7–15 dinner includes soup or salad, entrée and bread. For a few dollars more, you can sweeten the deal with a slice of cheesecake. Invitingly decked out with couches, chairs, fireplace and sun porch, the café also doubles as the common area for the complex.

Visitors to Yosemite will be hard-pressed to find an all-around better place to stay. Hikers can wake to a hot shower, eat a hearty breakfast, buy a box lunch and drive to the park in less than an hour. That's hard to beat.

~ fast facts ~

Dorm Rates: $15–18

Private Rooms: $40–70 (2–4 people with shared bath); $55–115 (2–5 people with private bath)

Season: all year

Office Hours: 7am–11pm

Lock-out: n/a

Size: 67 beds

Credit Cards: MasterCard, Visa, Discover

Network: HI

Beds: spring mattresses

Kitchen: yes

Bathrooms: shared, dorm-style for dorms; varies for privates

Lockers: yes, in dorms & café

Extras: onsite café, Internet access, hammocks, board games, campsites, ADA-accessible, laundry

Be Aware: crowded dorms

In The Area: Yosemite National Park hiking, biking and climbing, white water rafting, horseback riding

Local Tip: The onsite café is a good deal; 3-day Yarts bus pass is a better value than 3 RT bus tickets.

Closest Free Internet: unknown

Parking: free parking at hostel, which is an Amtrak and Greyhound stop (get ticket to "Merced"); Yarts bus from hostel to Yosemite National Park

is this hostel great for you?

SOLO WOMEN Yes. Many Bug guests fit this profile.

PARTY ANIMALS No. Wholesome atmosphere. Lots of families and hiking clubs.

OVER 30 Yes. Lots of opportunities to socialize in the café.

OVER 50 Yes. Do yourself a favor, though, and stay in a private room.

COUPLES Yes. Cozy private rooms have double beds.

FAMILIES Yes. Lots of room for kids to run around.

GROUPS Yes. Many groups are hosted here. Up to 120 can be accommodated in the ampitheater, ballroom & meeting room.

Montara, California

HI-POINT MONTARA LIGHTHOUSE
P.O. Box 737
16th Street, Highway One
Montara, CA 94037
Phone: (650) 728-7177
Fax: (650) 728-7177
E-mail: himontara@norcalhostels.org
Website: www.norcalhostels.org

~ what to expect ~

Short of boarding a boat, you just can't get any closer to the ocean than this.

Located in the residential buildings of a historic lighthouse, this hostel's setting makes it a must-visit destination for many travelers. The cliffside patio woos photographers, writers and daydreamers with dramatic ocean swells and crashing waves. The local community wisely capitalizes on this spirit, holding meditation and movement classes in one of the side buildings.

Guests will find the nautical hostel interior comfortable, but not especially noteworthy. The common areas include two newly painted kitchens, a dining room and a living room whose wood-burning stove chases the chill on winter nights.

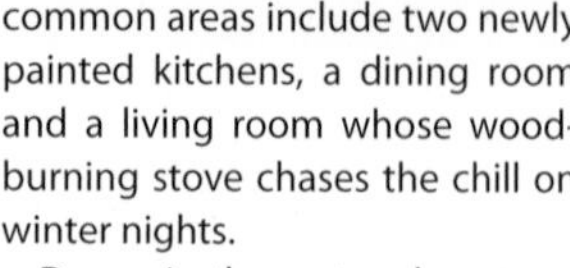

Dorms in the restored century-old building are clean but basic. One has an attached bath; the others share a hall bath. Each private room contains a dresser, desk, chair and bunk beds that sleep three. Two private rooms share a bath.

There are only three lighthouse hostels left in the United States. A visit to any of them is a visit you'll remember long after you're home.

~ fast facts ~

Dorm Rates: $18 HI members, $21 non-members

Private Rooms: $51 for 1–2 HI members, $57 for 1–2 non-members (bunk beds with queen on bottom, single above)

Season: all year

Office Hours: 7:30am–10am & 4:30pm–10pm

Lock-out: 10am–4:30pm

Size: 50 beds

Credit Cards: MasterCard, Visa, JCB

Network: HI

Beds: foam mattresses

Kitchen: yes – multiple

Bathrooms: house-style

Lockers: no

Extras: Internet access, wireless Internet access, wood-burning stove, free sleepsacks

Be Aware: reservations are a good idea in the summer

In The Area: beach surfing, kayaking, windsurfing, tide pools, Bikecentennial California Coast Bicycle Route

Local Tip: See the gray whale migration November–April. Private rooms are nicer here than at Pigeon Point.

Closest Free Internet: Half Moon Bay public library

Parking: free parking at hostel

is this hostel great for you?

SOLO WOMEN Yes. Good for a peaceful getaway.

PARTY ANIMALS No. This is an alcohol-free facility and there are no bars within walking distance.

OVER 30 Yes. Don't leave California without staying here or at Pigeon Point.

OVER 50 Yes. Private rooms are the way to go.

COUPLES Yes. Romantic atmosphere. Private rooms have great ocean views.

FAMILIES Maybe. Private rooms sleep three.

GROUPS Yes, if not too large. Two kitchens are available, but living room is only average in size.

Monterey, California

HI – MONTEREY (CARPENTERS HALL)
778 Hawthorne St.
Monterey, CA 93940
Phone: (831) 649-0375
Fax: n/a
E-mail: info@montereyhostel.org
Website: www.montereyhostel.org

~ what to expect ~

One of HI's newest hostels, Carpenters Hall fills a long-standing need of this popular tourist destination.

The Monterey Aquarium is just three blocks from the door. Adults and children will enjoy glimpsing life under the sea, and shows and exhibits can enthrall visitors for hours. There's plenty to enjoy after a visit to Monterey's main attraction, too. Specialty shops, antique stores, restaurants and art galleries line the streets of Cannery Row and of Old Monterey.

Convenient location may one of the most appealing aspects of this hostel. But there's a lot more to like. New sofas, chairs and lamps are grouped in small conversation areas in the large common room. The kitchen is modern and thoughtfully arranged.

The only negative aspect of the hostel is the dorms that sleep 7–16 people. This isn't an issue during the off-season when the rooms aren't full. But 15 roommates can make a good night's sleep hard to come by in the summer.

There are a couple of other quirks you should know about, too. First, you'll want to be sure to return by 11pm. This is one of the few hostels that still has a curfew. Miss it and you'll be locked out for the night. Second, the city's mandatory water rationing means you can't linger longer than six minutes in the shower. But most guests agree that the quality and convenient location of the accommodations far outweigh these small quirks.

~ fast facts ~

Dorm Rates: $23 HI members, $26 non-members

Private Rooms: $59–75

Credit Cards: MasterCard & Visa

Network: HI

Beds: foam mattresses in dorms, a mix of foam & spring mattresses in private rooms

Kitchen: yes, but no stove

Bathrooms: shared, dorm-style

Lockers: small ones in basement, larger ones outside

Curfew: 11pm

Extras: piano, discount coupons, information library, bike lockers

Be Aware: City water rationing means 6-minute showers; no stove in the kitchen.

In The Area: Monterey Aquarium, Cannery Row tourist area, museums, parks, whale watching, coastal drives

Local Tip: Skip the $8 17 Mile Drive. The view along Highway 1 is equally awesome. And it's free!

Closest Free Internet: Pacific Grove or Monterey public libraries

Parking: free parking at hostel

Season: all year

Office Hours: 8am–10:30am & 5pm–10pm

Lock-out: 10:30am–5pm

Size: 45 beds

is this hostel great for you?

SOLO WOMEN Yes. Be sure to make a reservation if you're coming for a festival (Steinbeck, Jazz, Blues, Seafood, Wine, etc.).

PARTY ANIMALS Yes. Cannery Row will keep you busy. Just don't forget about the curfew.

OVER 30 Yes. For a side trip, drive to upscale Carmel-by-the-Sea.

OVER 50 Yes. Choose a private room rather than the dorm.

COUPLES Yes, but not especially romantic.

FAMILIES Yes. Plenty to do, and the private rooms can sleep five.

GROUPS Yes. A group could rent out the large basement dorm (sleeps 16).

Pescadero, California

HI – PIGEON POINT LIGHTHOUSE
210 Pigeon Point Rd.
Pescadero, CA 94060
Phone: (650) 879-0633
Fax: (650) 879-9120
E-mail: pplhostel@norcalhostels.org
Website: www.norcalhostels.org

~ what to expect ~

Inspiring. Serene. Romantic. This hostel can be many things to many people. The only sure thing is that whatever it is to you is bound to be a good thing.

A cliff behind the hostel looms high above the crashing waves of the Pacific. And guests can relax in a hot tub on that cliff and soak in the drama unfolding below. It's one of my favorite spots in the world. The experience is so blissful, so five-star resort, you almost feel guilty that you're enjoying it at a hostel. Almost.

The hostel isn't as amazing as the setting and the area around the hot tub, but it works fine. Each of its three buildings houses two dorm rooms, one private room, a kitchen, living room and bathroom. The common rooms' matching furniture imparts the sense of a furnished apartment. Bedrooms are more basic: wood bunk beds and foam mattresses.

There isn't much nearby except the ocean. But Santa Cruz is only about a 30-minute drive. So you'll want to have transportation if you're going to spend more than one night at this hostel.

Play in the sun all day. Take in the sunset from the hot tub. Fall asleep to the sounds of the ocean. This is California at its best.

~ fast facts ~

Dorm Rates:	$18 HI members, $21 non-members
Private Rooms:	$51–57 (4 "couples rooms" with double bed; 1 family room with double bed & 2 sets of bunk beds)
Credit Cards:	MasterCard & Visa
Network:	HI
Beds:	foam mattresses
Kitchen:	yes
Bathrooms:	house-style
Lockers:	no
Season:	all year
Office Hours:	7:30am–10am & 4:30pm–9:30pm
Lock-out:	10am–4:30pm
Size:	52 beds
Extras:	piano, outdoor hot tub, lighthouse museum
Be Aware:	occasional seashore smells from ocean; lighthouse museum open only on weekends
In The Area:	whale watching, elephant seal viewing
Local Tip:	Call ahead to be sure hot tub is working.
Closest Free Internet:	Half Moon Bay public library
Parking:	free parking at hostel

is this hostel great for you?

SOLO WOMEN Yes. Not a place to visit just after a breakup, though.

PARTY ANIMALS No. This is an alcohol-free facility and there are no bars within walking distance.

OVER 30 Yes. Good place to read, write, think, not think.

OVER 50 Yes. Wrap up in a blanket and sit on the deck at night. The experience is unforgettable.

COUPLES Yes. The hot tub above the ocean is incredibly romantic.

FAMILIES Yes. One family room sleeps up to six.

GROUPS Maybe, depending on size. Each building sleeps 13–14 people at one time.

Sacramento, California

HI – SACRAMENTO (THE MANSION)
925 H St.
Sacramento, CA 94109
Phone: (916) 443-1691
Fax: (916) 443-4763
E-mail: hisac@norcalhostels.org
Website: www.hiusa.org

~ what to expect ~

Sacramento is a city that loves its hostel. Over a million dollars was spent to restore this old Victorian mansion to its original grandeur.

The massive white columns and wraparound front porch recall finer days. A gazebo and a little garden grace the back yard.

Step inside and you'll quickly see that the interior is just as beautiful as the exterior. A newer first-floor kitchen sports teal-accented yellow walls. Two sets of appliances are available: one at standard height and one at a level that's wheelchair-accessible. The living room, dining room and parlor are also on the first floor. They've all been redone in keeping with the period of the house's original glory days, and it's in these rooms that the hostel really shines. Rose-colored walls, crystal chandeliers, antique carpets, high ceilings with intricate molding create a very elegant setting. A massive wood staircase behind the front desk gracefully winds its way to the second floor.

The bedrooms are on the second and third floors. The dorms are adequate but don't live up to the expectations the first floor sets. While the second floor requires less climbing, the rooms on the third have more character. Built in the old attic, they retain its wood beams, high ceilings and exposed brick walls. The second-floor rooms are less interesting. The five private rooms are popular and should be reserved ahead of time.

The basement contains laundry facilities, lockers and a game room with a pingpong table and a dartboard. A meeting room is also available.

I'm happy to report that this hostel has eliminated the day-long lockout that meant guests weren't able to spend much time in the restored common rooms.

Cursed with a location that's fairly close to San Francisco yet not on the coast, Sacramento isn't a stop on most travelers' itineraries. But if you have an extra day, this could be a good place to spend it. Kids will enjoy Old Sacramento, the Western Gold Rush section of town, and adults can venture farther afield to explore nearby wineries.

Most hostels aren't lucky enough to get a $1.2 million restoration. Treat yourself to one that did.

~ fast facts ~

Dorm Rates:	$23.50 HI members, $26.50 non-members
Private Rooms:	$40 (single), $64 (shared bath), $75 (private bath)
Credit Cards:	MasterCard & Visa
Network:	HI
Beds:	foam mattresses
Kitchen:	yes – handicapped-accessible
Bathrooms:	shared, dorm-style
Lockers:	yes, but only 2 lockers in a room for 7 people
Season:	all year
Office Hours:	7:30am–10pm
Lock-out:	n/a
Size:	80 beds
Extras:	piano, pingpong table, dartboard, handicapped lift to upper floors
Be Aware:	No onsite Internet; hostel rents sleepsacks, not sheets; no locks on bedroom doors.
In The Area:	Old Sacramento Gold Rush town, wineries
Local Tip:	tasty food at the Tower Café
Closest Free Internet:	public library, 1 block away
Parking:	$5 secure parking at hostel; $10 shuttle from airport; bus and train stations nearby

is this hostel great for you?

SOLO WOMEN Yes. Beautiful building, but can be quiet.

PARTY ANIMALS No. This hostel doesn't draw a raucous crowd.

OVER 30 Yes. Wine connoisseurs will appreciate the nearby wineries.

OVER 50 Yes. The staff has been known to entertain guests with impromptu piano recitals.

COUPLES Yes, for a quiet getaway.

FAMILIES Maybe. The largest private room sleeps only three people.

GROUPS Yes. Meeting room available. Daytime rental possible.

San Diego, California

OCEAN BEACH INTERNATIONAL HOSTEL
4961 Newport Ave.
San Diego, CA 92107
Phone: (619) 223-7873 or
(800) 339-7263 in the U.S. & Canada
Fax: (619) 243-0093
E-mail: obihostel@aol.com
Website: www.californiahostel.com

~ what to expect ~

No one could accuse the Ocean Beach International Hostel of false advertising. One block from the beach, it couldn't be more international if it were a product of Central Casting. You'll hear English spoken here, but British or Australian accents are more in evidence than Texas drawls or New York staccato.

Dedicated to helping international visitors have a good time, the hostel requires guests to prove they fit the profile. A well-traveled current passport is typically used for validation. Americans are welcome, too, so long as they pass the same test.

If you have the credentials to get in, this is a fun place to stay. Located in a clean, non-touristy part of town, it bears no resemblance to the dirty crashpads you'll find at most California beachside hostels.

To ensure safety, guests must use an access code to open the front door at night. Every bedroom door has a lock.

Basic but clean, dorm rooms range in size from three to six beds. The sink and mirror in each room are added conveniences. All women's dorms have attached baths. Some men's dorms do, too. The few private rooms are comparably basic and feature twin beds or bunks.

Common hostel areas include a small kitchen with an eating area and a covered backyard patio that doubles as the TV room. But you'll find that the real party is out front. The covered front porch is the perfect spot for peoplewatching, especially when the Wednesday night markets set up shop right in front of the hostel.

Those traveling on a shoestring will appreciate the freebies: breakfast; coffee, tea and rice all day long; barbecue dinners twice a week; special parties from time to time. A Halloween party, complete with costumes and facepainting, introduces visitors to the national tradition.

This hostel isn't fancy. But it does a good job of providing travelers with a comfortable home-away-from-home experience.

~ fast facts ~

Dorm Rates:	$12–20, varies by season	**Season:**	all year
Private Rooms:	$18–25/person if sharing; $40 for 1	**Office Hours:**	8am–11pm (24-hour reception if you call first)
Credit Cards:	MasterCard & Visa	**Lock-out:**	n/a
Network:	Hostels America & Pacific Hostels Network	**Size:**	100 beds

Beds: spring mattresses

Kitchen: yes

Bathrooms: mix of house-style & dorm-style

Lockers: yes, with free locks

Extras: free breakfast, free barbecues (Tues. & Fri.), free VCR movies, free sheets, big-screen TV, laundry, beach chair, body board and beach umbrella rentals, Internet access

Be Aware: You MUST have proof of international travel to stay here. Free transportation from bus/train station/airport only if you call the hostel first to arrange it. Be early to breakfast or you might miss out.

In The Area: beach, restaurants, local bars, Sea World Amusement Park

Local Tip: free food samples at Wednesday night market

Closest Free Internet: public library

Parking: street parking; free transportation from bus station, train station or airport *if you call the hostel first*

is this hostel great for you?

SOLO WOMEN Yes, if laid-back.

PARTY ANIMALS Yes. Friendly people, alcohol permitted, no curfew.

OVER 30 Yes. Great beach location.

OVER 50 Maybe. People are nice and not too rowdy. But expect a younger crowd.

COUPLES Yes. Private rooms are available but pretty basic.

FAMILIES No. Too small and oriented toward a beach crowd.

GROUPS No. Too small.

San Diego, California

HI – SAN DIEGO, POINT LOMA
3790 Udall St.
San Diego, CA 92107
Phone: (619) 223-4778
Fax: (619) 223-1883
Website: www.hiusa.org
E-mail: pointloma@sandiegohostels.org

~ what to expect ~

Be sure to call ahead for reservations before heading to this hostel. Popular with both solo travelers and groups, it's frequently booked.

Everyone likes this smaller low-key hostel within walking distance of the ocean. The slow, relaxing pace of its residential neighborhood is just what most folks hope to find when they visit San Diego. Travelers who book themselves into one of the downtown hostels are usually pretty quick to try to move out here by the beach.

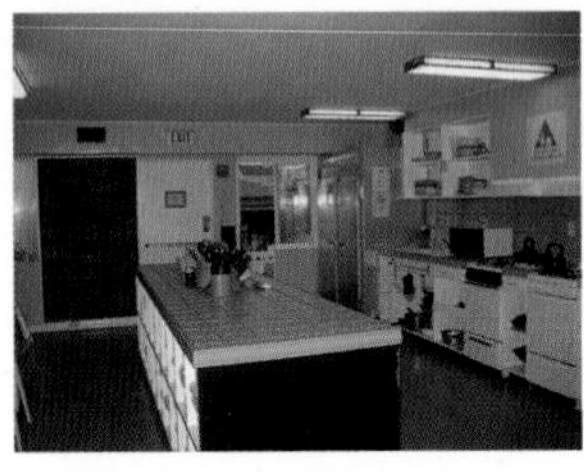

The building's floor plan has group appeal. First-floor common rooms all open and flow into each other. So there's plenty of elbow room for everyone. The kitchen has two stoves and a large, tiled island with enough counter space to prepare communal meals. The attached dining area features several round tables and chairs and an upright piano. If group sing-alongs aren't your cup of tea, however, you can always watch movies on the big-screen TV in the attached den.

Soft green walls and long white drapes lend the den a relaxing air. The other common areas are more playful. Shiny blue walls are decorated with maps, and event announcements keep guests posted on local happenings.

Upstairs, you'll find the bedrooms, each painted a different color. Private rooms are accessorized with coordinating curtains and quilts. Private room and dorm guests share hall bathrooms.

If surfing, swimming and sunbathing are the reasons you came to San Diego, you're in luck. Anyone at the front desk can point you in the right direction. Your feet will take it from there.

~ fast facts ~

Dorm Rates: $17–20 HI members, $20–23 non-members

Private Rooms: 11 private rooms $42 for 1 or 2 HI members, $45 for 1 or 2 non-members

Credit Cards: MasterCard, Visa, Discover, AMEX

Network: HI

Beds: spring mattresses

Kitchen: yes

Bathrooms: shared

Lockers: yes

Extras: TV, Internet access, laundry, highchair

Be Aware: frequently full – call ahead for reservations.

In The Area: beach, restaurants, local bars

Local Tip: Food samples at Wednesday night market are free.

Closest Free Internet: public library, 1 block away

Parking: street parking

Season: all year

Office Hours: 8am–10pm

Lock-out: n/a

Size: 53 beds

is this hostel great for you?

SOLO WOMEN Yes. Extremely safe residential neighborhood.

PARTY ANIMALS Not especially. Quiet atmosphere.

OVER 30 Yes. Comfortable private rooms.

OVER 50 Yes, if you don't mind the daytime lock-out.

COUPLES Yes. Double beds are available in private rooms.

FAMILIES Yes. A highchair and rocking chair are available for infants.

GROUPS Yes. The entire facility is frequently rented by groups.

San Francisco, California

THE ELEMENTS
2524 Mission St.
San Francisco, CA 94110
Phone: (866) 327-8407 or
(415) 647-4100
Fax: n/a
Website: www.elementssf.com
E-mail: reservations@elementssf.com

~ what to expect ~

The Elements is the best hostel in San Francisco.

A noticeable void had marred this city's hostelling scene. The City by the Bay had plenty of hostels. (I researched 15.) But none had what it took to warrant a solid recommendation. Given that more hostellers visit San Francisco than any other location in the United States, that was a very distressing state of affairs.

But there's no longer any reason to be distressed. The Elements has most everything I like to see in a hostel – and a generous helping of extras.

Ethnic, interesting and safe, the neighborhood is a hosteller's delight. This is a predominantly Latin area. References to El Salvador and Mexico abound in merchants' advertisements and this influence surrounds the hostel. Several colorful murals decorate nearby buildings and some of the city's best tapas restaurants are just around the corner. Additionally, a nighttime walk around the neighborhood confirmed locals' certainty of its safety. Streets are empty of the panhandlers, homeless people and scary sorts that you almost expect to find in cities these days. This part of town is a bit off most beaten tourist paths. However, a city bus stops out front and a subway station is just a couple of blocks away. You can use either type of transport to zip down to the wharf.

The hostel itself earns high marks, too. Each floor is painted a bright signature color and the brand-new facility has a clean, contemporary feel. Bedroom choices include dorms with just two sets of bunk beds or private rooms that have either one queen-size bed or one set of bunk beds. All of the beds have new spring mattresses. No foam cots here! Each bedroom also has a television and its own private bath. Bathrooms sparkle with polished silver hardware and bright white tiles. *(cont'd on p. 52)*

~ fast facts ~

Dorm Rates: $19–24

Private Rooms: $58 (twin bunks), $60 (queen-size bed)

Credit Cards: MasterCard & Visa

Network: n/a

Beds: spring mattresses

Kitchen: limited (microwave & refrigerator only)

Bathrooms: private, house-style

Lockers: yes

Season: all year

Office Hours: 24 hours

Lock-out: n/a

Size: 30 dorm beds & 7 private doubles

Extras: free Internet, free breakfast, free linens and towels, rooftop deck, in-room TV, laundry, onsite café/bar/restaurant

Be Aware: no dishes or stove in kitchen; $20 cash key deposit

In The Area: Edgy political murals reflect neighborhood ethnic heritages & issues; nearby public transport to Fisherman's Wharf and Alcatraz tours, Chinatown, Nob Hill, Haight-Ashbury district & Golden Gate park/bridge. Tours can be booked for Napa wine country and Yosemite National Park.

Local Tip: Popular Spanish tapas restaurants/bars on Valencia. This safe, working-class Latin neighborhood has recently been "discovered" by young white professionals who are buying up property.

Closest Free Internet: onsite

Parking: garage parking behind the hostel, subway 2 blocks away, bus stop in front of hostel

is this hostel great for you?

SOLO WOMEN Yes. Safe neighborhood.

PARTY ANIMALS Yes. Nice bar/restaurant attached to hostel.

OVER 30 Yes. Diverse, interesting part of the city.

OVER 50 Yes. Each room has a private bathroom.

COUPLES Yes. Private rooms with one queen-size bed available.

FAMILIES Yes. A family can use an entire 4-person dorm room.

GROUPS Yes. This is a large hostel, well-suited for groups.

Plans are underway to open a bar on the hostel rooftop, which has a grand view of the city. For the time being, it's very suitable for sunbathing. (This section of town is blessed with rays even when the rest of town is cloud-covered.)

As if the hostel and the location weren't enough, the owner provides guests with an abundance of extra services. Linens and towels are free, Internet access is free and a tasty continental breakfast is provided free of charge in the attached café. Guests can enjoy their breakfast indoors or carry it to one of the little outdoor tables. During the day, a light lunch can be purchased at the casual café. At night, however, a hip, two-story restaurant next door to the hostel commands all the attention. Dress to impress. Meal prices are too steep for hostellers, but it's a nice place to splurge on a drink. (The owner has even been known to distribute free drink coupons to hostel guests.) Both the café and restaurant/bar are open to the public.

The only section of the hostel that needs work is the kitchen, which takes minimalism to a whole new level. A microwave and refrigerator are available, but I didn't find a stove, sink, pots and pans or even dishes. The owner indicated that he intends to correct this deficiency. I'll overlook it for now, since he's done everything else just right.

~ best for sun & sand ~

HI- Santa Monica/Los Angeles
Los Angeles, CA

HI-Cadillac Hotel
Los Angeles, CA

Ocean Beach International Hostel
San Diego, CA

HI-San Diego
San Diego, CA

HI – Clearwater Beach
Clearwater Beach, FL

The Tropics
Miami Beach, FL

HI- Miami Beach
Miami Beach, FL

Pirate Haus
Saint Augustine, FL

HI- Galveston
Galveston, TX

Angie's Guest Cottage
Virginia Beach, VA

San Francisco, California

HI – FISHERMAN'S WHARF
Fort Mason, Building 240
San Francisco, CA 94123
Phone: (415) 771-7277
Fax: (415) 771-1468
E-mail: sfhostel@norcalhostels
Website: www.norcalhostels.org

~ what to expect ~

Because HI–Fisherman's Wharf has the safest and most convenient location, it should be first alternate hostel when The Elements is full. (Some may even make this their first choice, due to the fine location and free parking.)

The hostel sits in the back of the old Ft. Mason army base, next to a park. Just three blocks away is famed Fisherman's Wharf, the city's hub of tourist activity. A waterfront collection of shops and restaurants, the Wharf is also where tours depart for the historic Alcatraz Island prison and vintage cable cars pick up passengers on their way to Chinatown, Haight-Ashbury and North Beach.

This location exceeded my expectations. Unfortunately, the hostel itself failed to meet them. Always full in the summer, this urban enterprise appears to rely more on quantity than on quality. The hostel sleeps over a hundred guests at a time. A large dining area and two big kitchens easily accommodate groups. These rooms are modern and clean, but the basement location can give them a cold, cavernous feel at night.

Most upstairs rooms are worn and in need of freshening. The bedrooms are institutionally stark, devoid of decoration of any kind. No private rooms are available, and several of the dorms are quite large. And although the cleaning staff attends to them frequently, the bathrooms always feel like they're in need of a good scrubbing. A natural outcome of being housed in old military buildings, I suspect.

International solo travelers make up the largest percentage of Ft. Mason guests. As a result, the common areas seem filled with a true hostel community spirit. The remainder of the clientele includes groups – large and small – and young people new to San Francisco and in search of jobs and apartments.

All in all, this isn't the place to take a first-time hosteller. However, seasoned veterans will find the facility adequate & the location outstanding.

~ fast facts ~

Dorm Rates:	$23	**Season:**	all year
Private Rooms:	$69	**Office Hours:**	24 hours
Credit Cards:	MasterCard, Visa & JCB	**Lock-out:**	n/a
		Size:	170 beds

Network: HI

Beds: foam mattresses

Kitchen: yes

Bathrooms: shared, dorm-style

Lockers: yes

Extras: free continental breakfast, onsite café, Internet access, concierge desk, TV in café, secure bag storage available, free linens, laundry facilities

Be Aware: Parking lot is not secure, dressing area in women's bathroom is not very private.

In The Area: Fisherman's Wharf, Alcatraz prison, cable cars, Golden Gate Bridge and Park, Chinatown, museums, zoo, wine country tours, many restaurants and bars

Local Tip: Free walking tours are offered by City Guides. (www.sfcityguides.org)

Closest Free Internet: public library

Parking: free parking on Ft. Mason grounds

~ day trips ~

A worthwhile side trip from San Francisco is the nearby wine country. Tasting rooms in Napa Valley and Sonoma County offer award-winning red and white wines. It's typical to pay a small fee – usually around $5 – to taste up to half a dozen of each winery's wares. However, visitors centers can help you identify several that still offer free tastings. Unfortunately, there isn't any regular public transportation to the wine country. If you choose to drive, be sure to pace yourself: There are over 200 wineries in the valley. Or leave the driving to someone else and take a bus tour of the area. Any of the Sedobe-recommended hostels can help you make reservations.

San Francisco, California

HI – CITY CENTER
685 Ellis St.
San Francisco, CA 94109
Phone: (415) 474-5721
Fax: (415) 776-0775
E-mail: sfcitycenter@norcalhostels.org
Website: www.norcalhostels.org

~ what to expect ~

While the HI–Fisherman's Wharf hostel has a great location and a somewhat shabby interior, HI–City Center has a fabulous interior and a really shabby location.

HI's newest San Francisco hostel is a newly renovated old hotel. The lobby has been meticulously restored to its previous splendor. With antique high-back chairs and refinished wood panel doors in the sitting area and an intricate carved wood balcony above, it's a pleasant place to relax and chat with the front desk staff.

The dining area attached to the lobby was once the hotel bar, and the vintage solid oak bar adds Old World charm. A small television allows diners to catch up on the day's news over breakfast. Few guests choose to make use of this small area or the attached kitchen, however. San Francisco is known for its outstanding restaurants and most people want to evaluate that reputation for themselves.

As converted hotel rooms, the dorm rooms offer more privacy than most. Each sleeps just four guests and has an attached private bath. Bathrooms throughout this hostel shine with cleanliness. Private rooms are available with either one double bed or two twin beds.

The problem with this hostel is its location. City Center borders on the Tenderloin neighborhood – one of the worst in the city. If you choose to walk around at night, be sure to take extra precautions. And be prepared to dodge panhandlers, people sleeping on the sidewalks and generally unsavory sorts.

The Elements remains my hostel of choice in the city, but this hostel is a good back-up choice.

~ fast facts ~

Dorm Rates: $23 HI members, $26 non-members

Private Rooms: $67 HI members, $70 non-members (for 1 or 2 guests)

Credit Cards: Mastercard, Visa, Discover, JCB

Network: HI

Beds: spring mattresses

Kitchen: yes

Bathrooms: private, dorm-style

Lockers: no

Extras: Internet access, television, free linens and towels

Be Aware: very bad neighborhood, difficult parking

In The Area: San Francisco sights

Local Tip: The neighborhood on one side of the hostel is safer than the other: Ask the front desk for the safest walking route.

Closest Free Internet: public libraries

Parking: $12–18/day parking in garage

Season: all year

Office Hours: 24 hours

Lock-out: n/a, security card access to rooms

Size: 30 dorm beds & 7 private doubles

~ day trips ~

If you have extra time in San Francisco, Sausalito makes for a wonderful day trip.

This wonderful community is just a short drive across the Golden Gate Bridge or can be easily reached via the ferry from Fisherman's Wharf. The picturesque little town actually feels more European than Californian. A whole wheat bagel is a novel commodity here, while French and Italian pastries are abundant at the neighborhood cafés. Excellent seafood restaurants sit right on the water.

San Luis Obispo, California

HI – SAN LUIS OBISPO (HOSTEL OBISPO)
1617 Santa Rosa St.
San Luis Obispo, CA 93401
Phone: (805) 544-4678
Fax: n/a
E-mail: esimer@slonet.org
Website: www.hostelobispo.com

~ what to expect ~

Shops, cafés, art galleries, bars, an old mission and a riverfront park are just a few blocks from the front door of this hostel.

While SLO is a cool little college town, it's the vibe in the hostel itself that brings hostellers back again and again. Folks gather at the dining room table each morning to make and eat free sourdough pancakes and share stories. Afternoons might be spent at the beach with new friends, tasting wine at some nearby vineyards or checking out the mission or the shops in town. Evenings could include a walk through the weekly farmers' market or a laid-back night at the hostel.

Located in a residential neighborhood, the hostel still feels like a home. The small common room features high ceilings, plaster walls, a white brick fireplace, lace curtains, a faux Oriental rug and an upright piano. The house has 22 beds, including two dorm rooms and two private rooms. All the beds have real mattresses – a real treat after weeks of the thin foam substitutes. The bad news (for some) is that all dorms may be coed during your stay. Call ahead to check on the setup for the day you plan to visit.

SLO is a convenient stop for anyone touring the coast. But be prepared. Once you arrive, you may not want to leave.

~ fast facts ~

Dorm Rates: $20 HI members, $22 non-members

Private Rooms: $40–60 for 1 or 2, $10 for additional guests; $55–75 for family of 5

Season: all year

Office Hours: 7:30am–10am & 4:30pm–10pm

Lock-out: 10am–4:30pm

Size: 22 beds

Credit Cards: no

Network: HI

Beds: spring mattresses

Kitchen: yes

Bathrooms: shared, house-style

Lockers: yes – limited number

Extras: free pancake breakfast, stereo, fireplace, piano, Internet access

Be Aware: The dorms frequently become coed. Call ahead to check on current configuration.

In The Area: shopping, winetasting, beach 10 miles away

Local Tip: farmers' market/street fair on Thursday nights

Closest Free Internet: public library , 7 blocks away

Parking: free parking at hostel

is this hostel great for you?

SOLO WOMEN Yes. Very friendly environment; a great choice for solo travelers.

PARTY ANIMALS Yes. Main Street bars are within walking distance.

OVER 30 Yes. Laid-back, artistic town full of interesting people.

OVER 50 Yes. Social types will appreciate this place most.

COUPLES Yes. Nice private rooms available.

FAMILIES Maybe. A family room accommodates five people. However, noisy children would disrupt the hostel's vibe.

GROUPS No. Too small.

Santa Barbara, California

SANTA BARBARA TOURIST HOSTEL
134 Chapala St.
Santa Barbara, CA 93101
Phone: (805) 963-0154
Fax: (805) 963-0125
E-mail: n/a
Website: www.sbhostel.com

~ what to expect ~

Strolling along the streets of Santa Barbara , you might think you've wandered onto a movie set. There just might be more beautiful people in this little city than any other place in the country.

Needless to say, it's a great place to sip a cup of coffee and watch the world go by. It's also a great place to hit the town at night and make new friends, and the hostel is full of folks ready to make new friends. This is a very young and very social hostel.

The hostel is well-positioned for those looking to play. Located right in the middle of all the activity, it's just a couple of blocks from both the beach and the main drag. The beach is a busy one, with a skate park to occupy the kids and a pier where adults can talk long walks (or short trolley rides). Grown-ups looking for more action can head into town, where the streets are replete with upscale shops, restaurants and bars.

Most hostellers are out on the town at night. But some stick around and hang out to play pool in the common area during the day. It's a room with an incomprehensible decorating theme: bright gold walls, hardwood floors, a rattan-covered front desk, round '50s retro booths and a giant fake stone statue against the wall. But it's festive, if in a random way.

Perhaps the best architectural element is the front wall of windows that allow sunshine to spill into the room throughout the day. A free breakfast is served each morning in a booth below the windows. Booths along the back wall offer additional dining space. The kitchen attached to this room is extremely small and, typically, extremely messy.

Beyond the common rooms lie the bedrooms and baths. A couple of small private rooms are available. But most guests make use of the large, sometimes crowded dorms, where up to 12 people sleep on metal bunks. Everyone shares the dorm-style bathrooms.

The early read on this new place is mixed. On one hand, the upbeat, social atmosphere is undeniable. On the other hand, it's disheartening to find a messy kitchen and crumbling ceiling tiles in the first year of operation.

~ fast facts ~

Dorm Rates: $23 summer, $20 other seasons

Private Rooms: $49

Credit Cards: Mastercard & Visa

Network: n/a

Beds: spring mattresses

Kitchen: yes, small

Bathrooms: shared, dorm-style

Lockers: yes, in hall

Extras: pool table, free continental breakfast, Internet kiosk, wireless Internet access, bike and rollerblade rentals

Season: all year

Office Hours: 8am–2am

Lock-out: 2am–8am

Size: 70 beds

Be Aware: loud train passes by at 4am; some lingering unofficial ties to Banana Bungalow; be home by 2am or get locked out

In The Area: shopping, rollerblading, biking, whale watching

Local Tip: A ride on the State St. electric bus is only 25¢.

Closest Free Internet: unknown

Parking: free onsite parking, Amtrak station across the street, bus station within walking distance

is this hostel great for you?

SOLO WOMEN Yes, especially if you're lookin' to hook up.

PARTY ANIMALS Yes. You'll be amongst friends here.

OVER 30 Yes. Santa Barbara is a great town and this hostel is a great value.

OVER 50 No. A young crowd.

COUPLES Not especially.

FAMILIES No. Not a family atmosphere.

GROUPS Maybe, if you rent the entire facility. Tiny kitchen, though.

Santa Cruz, California

HI – SANTA CRUZ
321 Main St.
P.O. Box 1241
Santa Cruz, CA 95060
Phone: (800) 909-4776 or
(831) 423-8304
Fax: (831) 429-8541
E-mail: info@hi-santacruz.org
Website: www.hihostels.com

~ what to expect ~

This hostel is a lovely collection of cottages in a quiet residential neighborhood. Guests check in at the main house, where one kitchen and some bedrooms are located. Visitors not assigned to the main house will walk through the landscaped courtyard to one of the newer little cottages next door. That's where you'll find dorm rooms that are not too big, not too small. Pretty much just right. And the shared, private bathrooms resemble those you probably have at home. Each cottage also has its own little common room, nicely appointed and brightened by sun streaming through its many windows.

All hostellers also have access to the newest building. Completely dedicated to common space, it provides opportunities to socialize with those not staying in your cottage. The brand-new kitchen, combination dining-TV room, laundry room and attached patio built into this new space make it a great addition to an already good hostel.

Hostellers will find a lot to enjoy in this surfer-hippie town. Anyone who wants to ride the waves can rent a board, while spectators can watch the surfers from the beach.

A visit to the west side of town – where you'll find the beach, boardwalk, and hostel – feels like a step into a long-past era. The old-fashioned boardwalk is of the Atlantic City genre, complete with a small amusement park featuring a Ferris wheel and other rides.

A pedestrian-friendly business district on the other, revitalized, side of town is home to a bevy of boutiques, chain stores and coffee shops. Jugglers, comedians and a varied assortment of other street performers provide plenty of free entertainment to keep a hosteller happy.

One final note: To keep the neighbors happy, the hostel has a strictly enforced curfew. Have a good time in town, but be sure to return before 11:00pm. If you don't, you'll be sleeping on the street instead of in your comfy bed.

~ fast facts ~

Dorm Rates: $21 HI members
$24 non-members

Private Rooms: dorm rates plus $10–15 per room

Credit Cards: Mastercard & Visa

Network: HI

Beds: mix of spring and foam mattresses

Kitchen: yes, new

Bathrooms: shared, house-style

Lockers: yes

Extras: laundry, Internet access, cable TV

Be Aware: 11pm curfew – no exceptions!

Season: year-round

Office Hours: 8am–10am & 5pm–10pm

Lock-out: 10am–5am

Size: 42 beds

In The Area: beach, surfing, boardwalk, small amusement park

Local Tip: Check out the pedestrian-friendly downtown with shopping, galleries and cafés.

Closest Free Internet: Santa Cruz library

Parking: permits sold for metered street parking

is this hostel great for you?

SOLO WOMEN Yes. Cottages make for a social environment.

PARTY ANIMALS Maybe. Plenty of fun to be had in town, but 11pm curfew puts a damper on things.

OVER 30 Yes. Charming, modern facility.

OVER 50 Yes. Curfew slows and quiets things down at night.

COUPLES Yes. Privates available.

FAMILIES Yes. Family room sleeps four and kids will enjoy the boardwalk.

GROUPS Only if a smaller group.

Saratoga, California

HI – SANBORN PARK HOSTEL
15808 Sanborn Rd.
Saratoga, CA 95070
Phone: (408) 741-0166
E-mail:
Website: www.sanbornparkhostel.org

~ what to expect ~

This hostel is located deep inside a forested park. You'd never guess that "Silicon Valley," the Bay Area's high-tech mecca, is just a few miles away.

You'll find wood beams and a natural stone fireplace inside this fancy log cabin. The living room is furnished with several comfortable couches and an old piano. The adjacent dining room seats up to 20 people at one long table. The bedrooms all have bunk beds and can be used either as single-sex dorms or private/ family rooms. A private bathroom is either attached or next door to each bedroom. With a wealth of windows that look out to the tall redwood trees, the upstairs dorm room is especially pleasant.

Those in search of lively evening entertainment will want to head to downtown Saratoga, neighboring Los Gatos or the city of San Jose. However, most guests visit Sanborn to escape city life for a few days. This hostel is well-known and well-loved by its community and small groups of adults frequently use it for retreats. During my visits, I've been joined by a women's singing group and participants of a silent retreat. The members of the latter group weren't great conversationalists, but their presence definitely enhanced the serene atmosphere. Not many international travelers make it to Sanborn. But those exhausted from navigating city sprawls would find it a welcome change.

To help keep rates low, guests are encouraged to perform one small chore each morning. It seems like a fair exchange – you won't find better accommodations for this price. I would, however, prefer not to have to complete my chore and vacate the hostel by 9am. Even in California, a state known for its tough lock-out policies, 9am–5pm is a long time for the door to be barred.

~ fast facts ~

Dorm Rates: $14 HI members, $16 non-members, $7 children

Private Rooms: same as dorm rates

Credit Cards: no

Network: HI

Beds: foam mattresses

Kitchen: yes

Bathrooms: house-style

Lockers: no

Extras: piano, fireplace, laundry, inexpensive towel and sleepsack rental

Season: all year (Jan.–March only open Thurs.–Sat.)

Office Hours: 7am–9am & 5pm–10:30pm

Lock-out: 9am–5pm

Size: 39 beds, including 2 family rooms

Be Aware: 9am–5pm lock-out and 11pm curfew, small daily chores requested (but not required) of guests

In The Area: hiking, volleyball, pingpong, Stanford University, Tech Museum, Egyptian Museum, Museum of Art and Children's Museum in San Jose

Local Tip: Free Shakespearean plays are performed in the park during the summer (within walking distance).

Closest Free Internet: public library

Parking: free parking at hostel

is this hostel great for you?

SOLO WOMEN Yes. Very safe and comfortable, but can get really quiet.

PARTY ANIMALS No. No nearby bars and the 9am lock-out will kill you.

OVER 30 Yes. Relaxing, woodsy atmosphere.

OVER 50 Yes. A good night's rest.

COUPLES Not especially.

FAMILIES Maybe. Multiple rooms can accommodate families, but no returning mid-day for a nap.

GROUPS Yes. Good for adult groups – except for the daytime lock-out.

~ best for peaceful getaways ~

Bridge Street Inn
Cambria, CA

Davison Street Guesthouse
Mammoth Lakes, CA

HI – Point Montara Lighthouse
Montara, CA

HI – Pigeon Point Lighthouse
Pescadero, CA

HI – Sanborn Park
Saratoga, CA

HI – Friendly Crossroads
Littleton, MA

Shaker Woods at Point Comfort
Sanbornton, NH

Circle A Ranch
Cuba, NM

HI – Tibbetts Point Lighthouse
Cape Vincent, NY

HI – Seaside
Seaside, OR

HI – Weisel
Quakertown, PA

Bear's Den Hostel
Bluemont, VA

HI – Blue Ridge Mountain Hostel
Galax, VA

Colorado Hostels

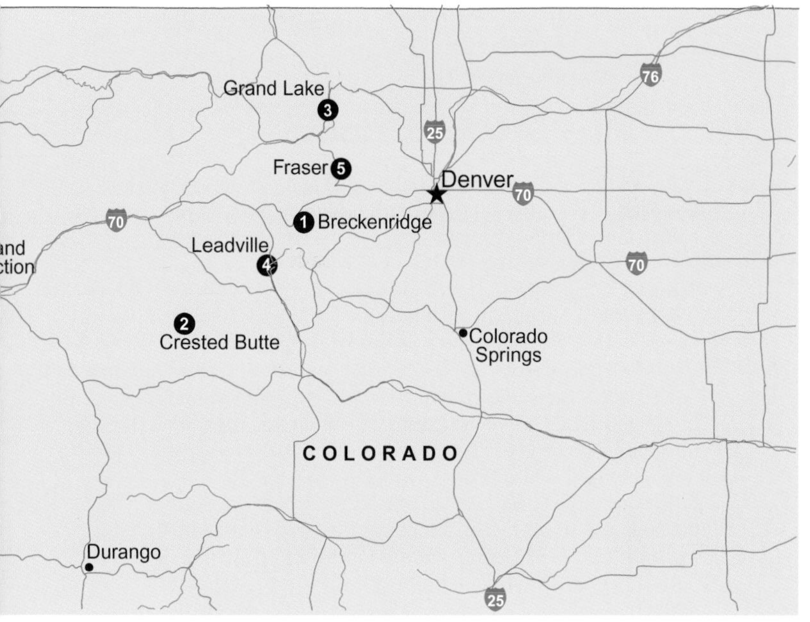

❶ **Breckenridge**
HI – Fireside Inn

❷ **Crested Butte**
HI – Crested Butte Intl. Lodge & Hostel

❸ **Grand Lake**
HI-Shadowcliff

❹ **Leadville**
Leadville Hostel and Inn

❺ **Winter Park/Fraser**
The Rocky Mountain Inn & Hostel

Breckenridge, Colorado

HI – FIRESIDE INN

P.O. Box 2252
114 North French St.
Breckenridge, CO 80424-225
Phone: (970) 453-6456
Fax: (970) 776-9577
E-mail: info@firesideinn.com
Website: http://www.firesideinn.com

~ what to expect ~

The Fireside Inn operates as both a B&B and a hostel. As a result, hostellers will find the inn to be much nicer than most. Anyone who's had an unfortunate experience at one of the slacker-crowd crashpads should give this place a try.

The inn is housed in a historic 1880 home. The character-rich ski-house decor includes antiques, leather furniture and a brick fireplace. Guests mingle in the living room and swap stories in the dining room, where breakfast is served by the owners, a friendly couple from England.

The price difference between the hostel and B&B accommodations is primarily based on the bedrooms. Hostel accommodations include four dorm rooms and two private rooms. All are clean and certainly adequate, but basic and very small. Each dorm has two sets of bunk beds; the private rooms sleep three in a bunk bed with a queen-size bed on the bottom and twin bed on top. During the busy winter season, one of the large upstairs B&B rooms is turned into a hostel dorm that sleeps 10 guests. The four hostel rooms downstairs share one private bath.

Whether you are a hosteller or a B&B guest, you can use the indoor hot tub. It's open until 8 o'clock each evening.

The inn is located in downtown Breckenridge, a busy resort town with much to offer. Bars, shops and restaurants to suit all tastes and budgets populate the business district. Because the town is located in the center of three popular ski resorts, winter is the busier season here. But winetastings, music festivals and a multitude of other events keep tourism alive in the summer. Really, there's no bad time to visit Breckenridge – or this hostel.

~ fast facts ~

Season: all year

Office Hours: 8am–9pm

Lock-out: no

Size: 12 beds

Dorm Rates: $32 HI members Jan.–April, $35 non-members
$22 HI members May–Nov., $25 non-members
$35 HI members Christmas week, $38 non-members

Private Rooms: $55–88, seasonal

Credit Cards: MasterCard & Visa

Network: HI

Beds: foam mattresses

Kitchen: kitchenette with microwave & refrigerator

Bathrooms: shared, house-style

Lockers: yes, very large

Extras: hot tub, free linens, ski work room, Internet access, continental or hot breakfast offered for $3

Be Aware: Reception is completely closed after 9pm: Call ahead for late arrival or you'll be out of luck.

In The Area: world-class ski resorts, shopping, restaurants, horseback riding, white water rafting,

Local Tip: "Sounds of Summer" music festival June–September. The Crown Tavern for coffee, wine, ice cream and live piano music on Saturday nights.

Closest Free Internet: public library

Parking: free lot parking, free ski season shuttle to Keystone, Copper Mt. & Frisco

is this hostel great for you?

SOLO WOMEN Yes. Very nice, safe neighborhood just blocks from Main Street.

PARTY ANIMALS Yes. Bars are nearby. Just be quiet once you return to the hostel.

OVER 30 Yes. This is a classy town and a classy hostel.

OVER 50 Yes. The mix of B&B and hostel rooms makes for a mellow clientele.

COUPLES Yes. Private hostel room has a queen-size bed. And be sure to take advantage of the indoor hot tub.

FAMILIES No. Hostel rooms are not designed for families.

GROUPS Yes, if small. In the winter, the family B&B room converts to a 10-person dorm.

Crested Butte, Colorado

HI – CRESTED BUTTE INTERNATIONAL LODGE & HOSTEL

P.O. Box 1332
615 Teocalli Ave
Crested Butte, CO 81224
Phone: (970) 349-0588
Fax: (970) 349-0586
E-mail: hostel@crestedbutte.net
Website: http://www.crestedbuttehostel.com

~ what to expect ~

Crested Butte is a funky little town. You'll not find it as busy as Breckenridge or Aspen, but the locals pride themselves on being different from those tourist centers. If you're a person who lives on a snowboard in the winter and a mountain bike in the summer, you'll fit right in.

The Crested Butte hostel bills itself as a "hostel for grown-ups" and I agree. I'd have no reservations about bring my non-hostelling friends to this ski lodge that still feels brand new inside.

The entire first floor of the building is devoted to the common areas – a large, light-filled living room, dining area and kitchen. Guests sleep in rooms on the second and third floors. Choices include dorm rooms with enough bunk beds to sleep two, four, six or eight people and private rooms with one double bed. Rooms are pretty basic, but each person does get an individual reading light. Those staying in a private room will find beds already made up and will receive free towels during their stay. A first-floor private room with private bath is handicapped-accessible.

The dorms all share dorm-style bathrooms. Individual dressing areas attached to the shower stalls add privacy. Some private rooms utilize those bathrooms; others have attached private baths. Everything is well-maintained and kept extremely clean.

This hostel gets a big thumbs-up.

~ fast facts ~

Dorm Rates: $18-25 HI members, $20-27 non-members

Private Rooms: $50–70

Credit Cards: MasterCard & Visa

Network: HI

Beds: spring mattresses

Kitchen: big enough for groups

Bathrooms: shared, dorm-style

Lockers: yes, in dorms

Extras: full-service laundromat next door, Internet access

Be Aware: Lock-out times change: Call ahead if that's important.

Season: all year

Office Hours: 8am–9pm

Lock-out: 1pm–4pm during some seasons: Call ahead.

Size: 51 beds

In The Area: skiing, mountain biking, hiking, white water rafting, fishing, dogsledding, sleigh rides

Local Tip: only a 12-mile hike to Aspen

Closest Free Internet: public library, 5 blocks away

Parking: free lot parking, free shuttle to ski slopes

is this hostel great for you?

SOLO WOMEN Yes. Can be quiet off-season, though.

PARTY ANIMALS Maybe. No alcohol allowed in hostel. Other mountain towns are livelier.

OVER 30 Yes. Especially if you're a snowboarder.

OVER 50 Yes. Bring your bike.

COUPLES Yes. Private rooms have queen-size beds.

FAMILIES Yes. The family room sleeps five.

GROUPS Yes. It's possible to rent the entire 50-bed facility.

Grand Lake, Colorado

HI – SHADOWCLIFF
405 Summerland Park Rd.
P.O. Box 658
Grand Lake, CO 80447
Phone: (970) 627-9220
Fax: (970) 627-9220
E-mail: judith@shadowcliff.org
Website: www.shadowcliff.org

~ what to expect ~

Situated on the west side of Rocky Mountain National Park, nestled in the pine trees and overlooking nearby Grand Lake, this hostel is in an ideal location for those who love the outdoors.

Shadowcliff is essentially a big mountain lodge. In this wood building whose windows look out in every direction, you never run the risk of forgetting where you are. A wraparound porch provides a tranquil place to sip a cup of coffee and gaze out at the lake in the morning. And after a day of hiking or boating, you can spend cool evenings curled up on a couch next to the fireplace.

Most accommodations are private rooms with a combination of double beds and bunk beds. A hosteller with a travel partner will want to opt for one of those rooms. If this hostel has a weakness, it's the accommodations for solo travelers. Just a few beds are available in small men's and women's dorms that are clean but crowded. An extra bank of sinks and mirrors has wisely been added to eliminate lines at the hall bathrooms all guests share.

This facility is especially suitable for groups. It houses a lot of people and has a sizeable kitchen, dining area and living space. It works equally well for a lively scout troop or as an adult retreat. In fact, seminars are sponsored and held at Shadowcliff. Visit their website for more information.

~ fast facts ~

Dorm Rates:	$15–20	**Season:**	June–October
Private Rooms:	$40 for 2, $11 each add'l person	**Office Hours:**	9am–9pm
Credit Cards:	MasterCard, Visa, Discover, AMEX	**Lock-out:**	n/a
Network:	HI	**Size:**	70 total beds (14 in dorms)
Beds:	spring mattresses in privates, foam mattresses in dorms		
Kitchen:	yes, small		
Bathrooms:	shared, dorm-style		
Lockers:	yes		
Extras:	fireplace, Internet access, deck with mountain views, seminars		

Be Aware: You must be able to climb several flights of stairs.

In The Area: Rocky Mountain National Park, hiking, biking, swimming

Local Tip: Kids will enjoy the Wild West theme present throughout the town of Grand Lake.

Closest Free Internet: public library, 4 blocks away

Parking: free onsite parking

is this hostel great for you?

SOLO WOMEN Yes. Expect tight quarters in the dorm, though.

PARTY ANIMALS No. This is not a place for you.

OVER 30 Yes. A peaceful, relaxing environment.

OVER 50 Yes. Just be prepared to climb stairs to the entrance and more to your room.

COUPLES Yes. Smaller private rooms will work for couples.

FAMILIES Yes. Family rooms are available.

GROUPS Yes. Especially well-suited to group outings and retreats.

Leadville, Colorado

LEADVILLE HOSTEL & INN
500 East 7th St.
Leadville, CO 80461
Phone: (719) 486-9334
Fax: n/a
E-mail: leadvillehostel@amigo.net
Website: www.leadvillehostel.com

~ what to expect ~

When "Wild Bill" bought this place a few years back, it was basically a dump. Then he and his partner, Kathy, completely renovated the mountain-house-turned-hostel. The improvements they wrought have resulted in enthusiastic word-of-mouth endorsements and repeat visitors.

Leadville's draw is definitely mountain scenery and outdoor activities. The area is full of "fourteeners" – mountains with an elevation over 14,000 feet – and most hostel guests are in town to hike and/or bike. Training begins in July for the "Leadville 100," a 100-mile race through the mountains. And the owners will be happy to give you a ride to the Colorado Trail trailhead, if you need one.

Given the variety of local activities, guests are usually exhausted by the end of the day. You'll generally find everyone hanging out and socializing in the TV room, where you can rest your weary bones on soft, comfy furniture grouped around a big-screen TV. If you decide to walk into town, grab a beer and soak up the Old West atmosphere at the Silver Dollar Saloon. This small mining town doesn't offer much else.

The hostel kitchen and dining room are large enough to accommodate small groups. Bedroom options include the fancy private rooms upstairs, where each room has a different arrangement of beds – doubles, twins and bunks – but all have B&B-style décor. Most have private baths. Campers have been known to use these rooms as honeymoon suites.

Those traveling solo, or on tighter budgets, will be sleeping downstairs in dorms that bunk 4-8 or in one of three small double-bedded private rooms. The basement doesn't have the charm of the upstairs rooms, but it's adequate. Downstairs guests share dorm-style bathrooms: Each one has three showers, sinks and toilets.

Interestingly enough, both times I visited this hostel, guests included equal numbers of 20-somethings and 50-somethings. Age just doesn't seem to matter once you put on your pack.

~ fast facts ~

Dorm Rates:	$15–20 (Get 7 nights for the price of 6.)
Private Rooms:	$45 for 1–2, $5 each add'l (private baths), $25 –30 for 1–2 (shared baths)
Credit Cards:	MasterCard & Visa (2% fee charged)
Network:	n/a
Beds:	spring mattresses
Kitchen:	yes
Bathrooms:	varies
Lockers:	yes, in dorms
Extras:	big-screen TV, videos, laundry, free linens, on-site massage, Internet access, group meals available
Be Aware:	dog-friendly; marathon & bike racers fill the hostel in August.
In The Area:	skiing, hiking, kayaking, mountain biking, river rafting
Local Tip:	Columbine Café for breakfast, $5.95 filet mignon dinners at Quincy's, best dinner value at Tennessee Pass Café, cheaper skiing at Ski Cooper
Closest Free Internet:	Lake County public library
Parking:	free parking for cars or buses, $40 shuttle service to Denver/Colorado Springs, $10 shuttle from Vail and Frisco (Winter Park) bus station, shuttles to hiking/biking trailheads available

Season:	all year
Office Hours:	24 hours
Lock-out:	n/a
Size:	22 beds

is this hostel great for you?

SOLO WOMEN Yes. Lost of interesting solo hikers & bikers here.

PARTY ANIMALS No. This town of 2,000 doesn't have much nightlife.

OVER 30 Yes. A rare hostel where the average age is over 30.

OVER 50 Yes. Several of the regulars are 60-year-olds practicing for the Leadville 100.

COUPLES Yes. Several cheap "couples rooms" are available.

FAMILIES Yes. The private rooms sleep families of various sizes.

GROUPS Yes. Group meals can be arranged and bus parking is available.

Winter Park/Fraser, Colorado

THE ROCKY MOUNTAIN INN & HOSTEL
15 CR 72, Box 600
Fraser, CO
Phone: (866) 467-8351 or
(970) 726-8256
Fax: n/a
E-mail: n/a
Website: www.therockymountaininn.com

~ what to expect ~

If I were to design and build my own hostel, I'd model it after the Rocky Mountain Hostel.

Experienced hostellers will be able to tell right away that the building was specifically designed to be a hostel. Each of the common areas has an open floor plan. The kitchen has a large center island for food preparation and a separate sink for washing dishes. The Mission-style dining table nearby seats 10. The adjacent high-ceilinged living room opens onto a deck with outstanding mountain views. Track lighting, modern furniture and live plants add the finishing touches.

Dorm rooms are also a pleasant surprise. All of the beds are very comfortable and are pre-made with pretty linens and comforters. Most are twins, but a few are bunk beds. Dorms sleep 4–6. One dorm has a queen-size bed and one set of twin bunks. That room has its own TV and DVD player and is often used by families. Guests are asked to use the huge lockers in each dorm, even if they don't lock up their belongings. As a result, the rooms stay tidy. All hostellers share four bathrooms with showers and changing areas.

High season is this area is winter, when people from around the world come to ski and snowboard. Proximity to Rocky Mountain National Park also makes this a good base for summer hiking and biking.

The hostel opened for business in 2002, but looks like it was finished yesterday. The owners add a little bit more each year and everything looks brand new. It's refreshing to visit a hostel that improves, rather than deteriorates, as the years pass.

~ fast facts ~

Dorm Rates: $19–30, seasonal

Private Rooms: no private hostel rooms; B&B rooms for $59–129

Credit Cards: MasterCard & Visa

Network: n/a

Beds: spring mattresses on most twin beds, a few bunk beds

Kitchen: new, large, well-stocked with community food

Season: all year

Office Hours: 8am–10pm

Lock-out: n/a

Size: 22 beds , plus 6 private rooms

Bathrooms: private bathrooms & shower/dressing rooms

Lockers: yes, very large lockers in all bedrooms

Extras: linens & towels provided, free DVD movies, color TV, laundry facilities with free detergent

Be Aware: Everyone pays a one-time $3 linen fee; reservations are highly recommended during the busy ski season.

In The Area: skiing, snowboarding, snow tubing, hiking, biking, golf, rafting, fishing

Local Tip: Summer is pretty quiet except for July's Rockfest and "Hawgfest" weekends (rock concerts and Harley Davidson gathering, respectively).

Closest Free Internet: Fraser Public Library

Parking: free onsite parking, ski shuttle, $50 shuttle from Denver airport, walking distance to Greyhound & Amtrak stations

is this hostel great for you?

SOLO WOMEN Yes. The owners are friendly and quick to recommend hiking trails, etc.

PARTY ANIMALS Yes in winter, no in summer.

OVER 30 Yes. This is a very classy hostel.

OVER 50 Yes. Visit during the summer season for a more serene experience.

COUPLES Not unless you can afford one of the fancy B&B rooms.

FAMILIES Yes. One room is perfect for a family of four and quiet hours help calm things down.

GROUPS Yes. Common areas are open and well-suited to groups.

~ best for hikers ~

Grand Canyon International Hostel
Flagstaff, AZ

The Yosemite Bug
Midpines, CA

HI – Fireside Inn
Breckenridge, CO

HI – Shadowcliff
Grand Lake, CO

Leadville Hostel
Leadville, CO

The Rocky Mountain Inn & Hostel
Winter Park/Fraser, CO

HI – Harper's Ferry Lodge
Knoxville, MD

HI – White Mountains
Conway, NH

High Peaks Hostel
Lake Placid, NY

HI – Seaside
Seaside, OR

Uncle Johnny's Nolichucky Hostel
Erwin, TN

Laurel Fork Lodge
Hampton, TN

Bear's Den Hostel
Bluemont, VA

District of Columbia (D.C.) Hostels

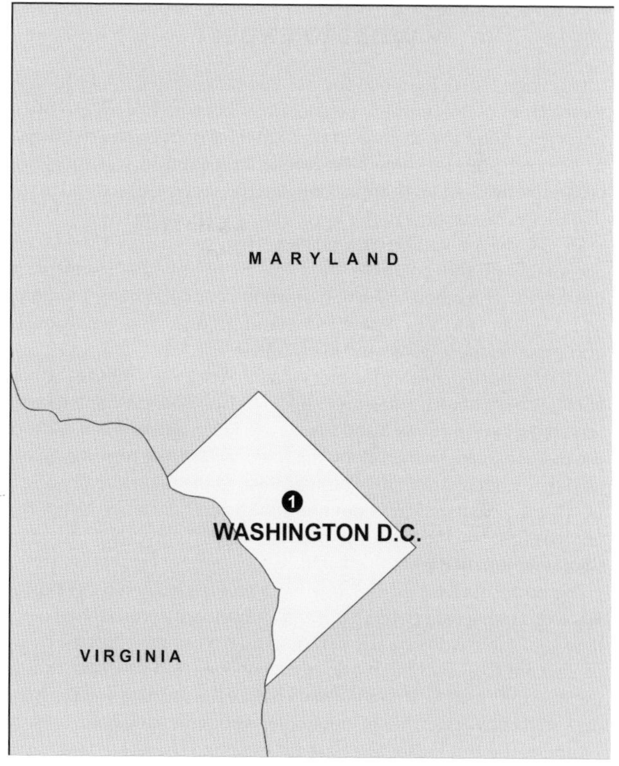

❶ **Washington, D.C.**
HI – Washington D.C.

Washington, D.C.

HI – WASHINGTON D.C.
1009 11th Street, NW
Washington, DC 20001
Phone: (202) 737-2333
Fax: (202) 737-1508
E-mail: reserve@hiwashingtondc.org
Fax: www.hiwashingtondc.org

~ what to expect ~

Washington, D.C. is unique and absolutely fascinating. I love to sit in the galleries of the House or Senate. We've become so cynical – many times with good reason – that it's easy to think of government officials as nameless, faceless, interchangeable. So it's fun to watch elected representatives get up to argue for issues they believe in and sad to see that they're often addressing rows of empty seats. (Who knew?)

So, OK, maybe you aren't a politico. Then spend your time taking advantage of the country's best free museum, the Smithsonian Institution. It's a whole collection of world-class collections, programs and exhibits. Air and Space. American History. The Smithsonian encompasses these jewels and many others.

Other great free sites are the memorials that pay silent tribute to Abraham Lincoln, Thomas Jefferson, Franklin Delano Roosevelt and all who served during World War II and the wars in Korea and Vietnam. Most of the memorials are located along the National Mall, the tree-lined parkland that stretches from the Potomac River to the Capitol. Every one is worth a visit, but walking from one site to another can be tiring. The one-day ticket on the Old Town tourist trolley isn't cheap ($30), but it's a smart investment if you can afford it.

The hostel itself is best described as a professionally run city hostel. You aren't going to find the charm and ambiance of a rural 40-bed place here, and there won't be any parties around a campfire. But it's clean, convenient to everything previously mentioned and very safe. Guests use a security card to access the main part of the building and the front desk staff does a good job of monitoring who comes and goes.

Groups use this hostel as a base for exploring the city. A large two-refrigerator, two-stove kitchen makes it easy to fix communal meals, and an equally large dining room makes it easy to serve and eat them. A big-screen television is the focal point of the common room.

Other hostel guests are businessmen and women in town to do business with one of the many government or not-for-profit organizations. The hostel's location makes it a good base for either endeavor. The only downside for business travelers is the absence of private rooms.

~ fast facts ~

Dorm Rates: $29 HI members, $32 non-members

Private Rooms: $69–$82

Credit Cards: MasterCard & Visa

Network: HI

Beds: foam mattresses

Kitchen: new large kitchen

Bathrooms: shared, dorm-style

Lockers: in some rooms

Extras: free coffee, juice and muffins each morning, laundry, Internet access

Season: all year

Office Hours: 24 hours

Lock-out: n/a

Size: 280 beds

Be Aware: not many programs or tours offered at the hostel

In The Area: White House, Congressional buildings, Smithsonian Museums, monuments, war memorials

Local Tip: Smithsonian Museums and Supreme Court tour are free.

Closest Free Internet: public library, 7 blocks away

Parking: parking lot across from hostel – $10/day, free street parking 6:30pm–7am

is this hostel great for you?

SOLO WOMEN Yes. Tough to meet people, though.

PARTY ANIMALS Not especially, although the city can be fun.

OVER 30 Yes. Lots of amazing stuff to see in town.

OVER 50 Yes. All ages are here due to the business clientele.

COUPLES No. No private rooms.

FAMILIES No. No private rooms.

GROUPS Yes. Many groups are hosted here.

"The world is a traveler's inn."
– *Afghan folk saying*

Florida Hostels

1 Clearwater Beach
HI – Clearwater Beach

2 Florida City
HI – Everglades

3 Miami Beach
HI – Miami Beach (Clay Hotel)

4 Miami Beach
The Tropics

5 St. Augustine
Pirate Haus

Clearwater Beach, Florida

HI – CLEARWATER BEACH
606 Bay Esplanade
Clearwater Beach, FL 33767
Phone: (727) 443-1211
Fax: (727) 443-1211
E-mail: magillrl@juno.com
Website: www.hiusa.org

~ what to expect ~

Clearwater Beach is on the west side of Florida. The mellow side. Where Miami is a hotbed of fast-paced activity, Clearwater Beach has a more relaxed, tropical island vibe.

This hostel is a good place to spend a vacation. Guests typically wake up and walk to the beach, hang out by the pool or borrow a canoe and explore the nearby islands. In the evening, everyone gathers at tables under thatched-roof outdoor umbrellas, laughing and telling stories. Cheap weekly barbecues provide a hearty meal that typically includes salad, coleslaw and grilled fish.

The indoor common area is really one big room with a small kitchen on one side and a small den on the other. Size doesn't matter, though. No one comes to Florida to stay indoors. The outdoor courtyard is really where the action is.

Sleeping options include one efficiency apartment and several private rooms, some with private kitchens and/or bathrooms. Guests can also choose between coed and gender-segregated dorm rooms with bunk beds. Most rooms are small, with equally small private baths attached.

Because the relaxed, homey atmosphere and safe neighborhood often leave guests disinclined to lock doors, it would probably be smart to stash your valuables in one of the coin-operated lockers. But you needn't fear that cleanliness will suffer as a result of the hostel's relaxed atmosphere. I can attest that all rooms are cleaned daily.

The owner of this hostel comes from a family with a good deal of hostel experience – both as guests and as owners. All that experience has definitely paid off for guests. Beneath the mellow atmosphere, you'll find unique amenities and an attention to detail that demonstrate a true commitment to hostellers.

~ fast facts ~

Dorm Rates: $14–15

Private Rooms: $39–43

Credit Cards: MasterCard & Visa

Network: HI

Beds: spring mattresses

Kitchen: small and cramped

Bathrooms: private, house-style

Lockers: yes

Extras: swimming pool, free canoes, shuffleboard, bike rental, bbq dinners, Internet, free use of community recreation center, laundry

Season: all year

Office Hours: 9am–noon & 5pm–9pm

Lock-out: n/a

Size: 33 beds

Be Aware: Spring Break belongs to teenagers.

In The Area: beach, Cuban Ybor City neighborhood and clubs in Tampa, Salvador Dali museum in St. Petersburg

Local Tip: early bird specials at Crabby Bill's, Port Corner Pizza, summer live music at park

Closest Free Internet: public library 6 blocks away

Parking: free, onsite parking; beach Jolly Trolley

is this hostel great for you?

SOLO WOMEN Yes. Enjoy the relaxed, friendly encounters that develop at the picnic tables under the thatched roof.

PARTY ANIMALS Yes. Spring Break is busiest; otherwise check out Ybor City.

OVER 30 Yes. Use the free canoes to explore the nearby islands.

OVER 50 Yes. The beach is within walking distance.

COUPLES Yes. Nice private rooms are available.

FAMILIES Yes. Small families will enjoy the pool, beach and canoes.

GROUPS No. Too small.

Florida City, Florida

HI – EVERGLADES
20 SW 2nd Ave.
Florida City, FL 33034
Phone: (305) 248-1122 or
(800) 372-3874
Fax: (305) 245-7622
E-mail: gladeshostel@hotmail.com
Website: www.evergladeshostel.com

~ what to expect ~

Swamp tours and alligator farms aren't the first things that come to mind when you think of Florida? A trip to the Everglades may change that.

Located in southern Florida, this is a fun stop between Miami Beach and the Keys. Renting canoes, kayaks and bicycles, the hostel makes it easy to explore this unique area on your own. It also offers tours for those who prefer to have someone else handle the ins and outs of getting to and from local points of interest. Whether you take a tour or venture out independently, your destinations are likely to be the same — the swamps of the Everglades National Park and one of the nearby alligator farms. If you have some extra cash, an airboat ride is a truly unique experience. The boats sit so high, they can maneuver in only a few inches of water; rides are available at any alligator farm.

Arriving back at the hostel after a day of fun, you're likely to be invited to join a communal dinner. This hostel does a great job of striking the balance between privacy and community. One building houses common areas — a kitchen, TV room and small library with an Internet-accessible computer. Another building houses the bedrooms, bathrooms, a kitchenette and a small sitting area that's a perfect place for that first cup of morning coffee before you're ready face the world.

The dorms are good-size and have the world's best bunk beds. Handcrafted of hard wood, the bunks have been designed with plenty of head space for the bottom bunk and an easy-to-climb step ladder for the top bunk. They're also outfitted with extra-comfortable mattresses. Those traveling with companions will get a kick out of the private rooms. Decorated with bright paint and fabric, each has its own theme – fire, water, etc.

The back yard features a barbecue grill and gazebo. A freshwater swimming area is in the offing.

Not many people are familiar with this area of Florida, but it's worth a visit. After all, your vacation photo album simply won't be complete without a picture of you holding a baby alligator!

~ fast facts ~

Dorm Rates:	$10-11 HI members, $13–14 non-members
Private Rooms:	$30-32 HI members, $33–35 non-members
Credit Cards:	MasterCard & Visa
Network:	HI
Beds:	spring mattresses (really comfortable!)
Kitchen:	yes, small
Bathrooms:	shared, house-style
Lockers:	no
Extras:	tours, canoe rental, kayak rental, bike rental, free Internet access, occasional group dinners, gazebo, barbecue, air conditioning, TV, laundry
Be Aware:	significant long-term clientele
In The Area:	swamp tours, alligator farms, canoeing, airboat rides, Everglades National Park, snorkeling & sailing
Local Tip:	amazing fruit stand on the way to the Park
Closest Free Internet:	onsite
Parking:	free onsite parking, pick-up from bus station available, shuttle to Everglades Park

Season:	year-round
Office Hours:	9am–9pm
Lock-out:	n/a
Size:	45 beds

is this hostel great for you?

SOLO WOMEN Yes. Friendly folks & communal meals.

PARTY ANIMALS No. Pretty quiet here.

OVER 30 Yes. Fun, themed private rooms.

OVER 50 Yes. Air conditioning keeps things comfortable.

COUPLES Yes. Check out the gazebo for privacy.

FAMILIES Yes. The kids will enjoy the nearby alligator farms and airboat rides.

GROUPS Yes. Works best if renting the entire facility.

Miami Beach, Florida

HI – MIAMI BEACH (CLAY HOTEL)
1438 Washington Ave.
Miami Beach, FL 33130
Phone: (305) 534-2988
Fax: (305) 673-0346
E-mail: info@clayhotel.com
Website: www.clayhotel.com

~ what to expect ~

The Clay Hotel is the first of two recommended hostels in Miami Beach. It's a good thing both exist, because this is a popular hostelling destination. This facility sleeps over 300 guests, but reservations are an absolute necessity during the January–May tourist season.

Visitors will find Miami Beach to be the ultimate in sophisticated beach living. When American movie stars, models and music artists aren't in Los Angeles or New York, they're in Miami. As a result, you'll find amazing restaurants, clubs and boutiques here. But just as in L.A. and New York, expect to find everything quite expensive.

The two recommended hostels are in a great location very close to each other. It's a clean, safe area two blocks from the water and right in the middle of all the action. Million-dollar hotels occupy some of the adjoining real estate.

You'll know you've arrived at the hostel when you spot an oversized plastic flamingo in front of a pink stucco building. This hostel definitely fits in with the 1940s Art Deco design popular in the area.

The two hostels' prices and amenities are very similar, but dorm rooms here may be preferable to those at The Tropics. Each dorm room is furnished with 2–4 sets of twin bunk beds. The rooms are all air-conditioned and each is outfitted with a small refrigerator.

However, if you are interested in a private room, I recommend The Tropics over the Clay Hotel. This is largely due to price. The rooms are equally nice in both locations, but much less expensive at The Tropics. If you choose to stay in a private room here, you can choose between economy, standard, deluxe or VIP rooms with varying levels of amenities and degrees of bathroom privacy. Every room has a TV, local phone, air conditioning and a small refrigerator. VIP rooms have balconies.

The common room and kitchen are very basic. There are plastic chairs in the common room and the only dining table is outside.

The attached restaurant and bar, however, are unique to this hostel and are great places to hang out and meet fellow travelers. They're the main reason I'd choose this hostel.

~ fast facts ~

Dorm Rates: $17 HI members, $19 non-members

Private Rooms: $41–88 HI members, $43–90 non-members

Credit Cards: MasterCard & Visa

Network: HI

Beds: spring mattresses

Kitchen: small

Bathrooms: dorm-style

Lockers: yes, wallet-size

Extras: onsite restaurant and bar, free linens and towels, Internet, laundry

Be Aware: $10 key deposit

In The Area: beach, shopping, restaurants, clubs

Local Tip: A market sets up next door on weekends.

Closest Free Internet: public library

Parking: city parking typically $10–15

Season: all year

Office Hours: 24 hours

Lock-out: n/a

Size: 300 beds

is this hostel great for you?

SOLO WOMEN Yes. Lots of fun to be had.

PARTY ANIMALS Yes. Miami is made for party animals, and this hostel has an attached bar.

OVER 30 Yes. Check out the clubs in town and try a little salsa dancing.

OVER 50 Yes. Stay in a luxury neighborhood without the luxury prices.

COUPLES Yes. Some private rooms have full-size beds.

FAMILIES No. No family rooms available.

GROUPS Yes. This 300-bed facility can easily accommodate groups.

Miami Beach, Florida

THE TROPICS
1550 Collins Ave.
Miami Beach, FL 33139
Phone: (305) 531-0361
Fax: (305) 531-8676
E-mail: mail@tropicshotel.com
Website: www.tropicshotel.com

~ what to expect ~

The Tropics is the second of two recommended hostels in Miami Beach. Both are in the white-hot South Beach neighborhood, home to the rich and famous. You can't be in a better location.

Miami is permeated by a very strong Latin influence. You'll sense it in the people, the music, the food and the cocktails. That intensity combines with the heat of the sun to create a passionate, exciting atmosphere.

Even those who don't typically stay in hostels will feel comfortable in the private rooms in The Tropics. This hostel accommodates 2-4 people in rooms with one double bed, two double beds, two twin beds, three twin beds or one double bed and one single bed. Two people who share a $39 private room at The Tropics are truly taking advantage of the best deal in town. You won't be sacrificing quality for value, either. The freshly painted rooms are decorated in a cool, minimalist black-and-white scheme. Each one has air conditioning, cable TV, a phone, reading light and attached private bathroom. In addition to typical bedroom furniture, each room also has two chairs and a small glass table for dining. If you ask, you can get a room with a view of the downstairs pool.

Dorm rooms are more basic, but are comfortable and are cleaned daily. Each room holds 4-8 guests; all have air conditioning and attached bathrooms.

The only deficiencies in this hostel are in the indoor common area. The lobby, which serves as the only common area, has several chairs but little else. Most cooking is done outdoors. The refrigerator and microwave are inside, but the stove is outside. The only dining area is also outside. This adds to the tropical atmosphere in nice weather, but can be a problem in the rain. Luckily, Florida receives a lot more sunshine than rain.

You can enjoy the rays without leaving the hostel, which sports an Olympic-size swimming pool. But most guests choose to visit the beach, which is just a few blocks away.

~ fast facts ~

Dorm Rates: $16–24

Private Rooms: $50–100 (1 or 2)
$62–112 (3)
$75–125 (4)
(online discounts)

Credit Cards: MasterCard & Visa

Network: n/a

Beds: spring mattresses

Kitchen: Yes, stove is outside.

Bathrooms: private, house-style

Lockers: yes, wallet-size

Season: all year

Office Hours: 24 hours

Lock-out: n/a

Size: 66 dorm beds plus 54 private rooms

Extras: swimming pool, free linens, air conditioning, grill, fax service, tour information

Be Aware: valid passport required to stay in dorm; outdoor kitchen; no blankets

In The Area: beach, shopping, restaurants, clubs

Local Tip: Pick up the hostel newsletter for coupons.

Closest Free Internet: Fraser Public Library

Parking: city parking typically $8–10/day; airport shuttle available

is this hostel great for you?

SOLO WOMEN Yes. Hang out by the pool to make friends.

PARTY ANIMALS Yes. South Beach is one big party!

OVER 30 Yes. Perfect base for sightseeing.

OVER 50 Yes. Each room has a private, attached bathroom.

COUPLES Yes. "Good couples rooms."

FAMILIES Yes. Private rooms accommodate up to four people.

GROUPS Yes. This large hostel can easily accommodate groups.

St. Augustine, Florida

PIRATE HAUS
32 Treasury St.
St. Augustine, FL 32084
Phone: (904) 808-1999
Fax: (904) 808-1999
E-mail: great@piratehaus.com
Website: www.piratehaus.com

~ what to expect ~

The Pirate Haus markets itself as "fun European-style lodging" and a "self-serve B&B." Those terms do a good job of conveying the fun to be had at this hostel. This marketing strategy also helps the owner attract guests who've never heard of hostelling.

Expanding the network of hostellers is a worthy goal and the Pirate Haus is the right kind of hostel to accomplish it. The previous owners spent many years as hostel managers before opening the Pirate Haus. Their experience and commitment to hostellers were evident in the personal attention they provided their guests. It's always a bit scary when a really good hostel changes hands. However, hostellers are reporting that the new owner is doing a great job of maintaining the high standard that regulars have grown to expect and newcomers appreciate.

Guests enjoy the fun décor and spotless rooms that the Pirate Haus offers. The five private rooms are more like inexpensive B&B rooms. All are nicely decorated and have hardwoods floors, air conditioning and small refrigerators. One room has a full-size bed; each of the others sleeps four. There's no need to bring linens: Beds in all private rooms are made up prior to guests' arrival. Solo travelers will find that the dorms house comfortable wooden bunks in air-conditioned rooms. These rooms aren't as fancy as the private quarters, but they're more than adequate.

Common areas include a kitchen, den and rooftop patio. The table in the small kitchen seats six, but most folks gather across the hall in the den. A life-size wooden pirate stands in a corner of this room. Pastel walls, nice furniture and live plants complete the scene as guests share stories, watch TV and play board games.

The hostel is conveniently located in the heart of the "old city" section of St. Augustine. The town can be good fun. Horse-drawn carriages traverse cobblestone streets and costumed characters guide tours of historic buildings. Be aware, however, that a multitude of T-shirt shops and souvenir stands can detract from the otherwise quaint town.

~ fast facts ~

Dorm Rates:	$18 (Note: Children under 13 stay free in private rooms; discounts for cross-country bicyclists.
Private Rooms:	$47–60
Credit Cards:	MasterCard & Visa
Network:	VIP, Hostels Americas
Beds:	foam mattresses
Kitchen:	small, but sufficient
Bathrooms:	mixed.
Lockers:	yes
Season:	all year
Office Hours:	8am–10am & 5pm–10pm
Lock-out:	n/a
Size:	22 beds plus private rooms
Extras:	free pancake breakfast, gas grill, discounts to local restaurants and tours, rooftop patio, free Wi-Fi Internet access for laptops
Be Aware:	Town gets pretty quiet after 5pm; one dorm is coed.
In The Area:	historic cobblestone district, Castillo fort, Catholic shrine, oldest house and schoolhouse in the U.S., beach
Local Tip:	Jr. Ranger program for children at the fort; Fountain of Youth attraction not worth the money.
Closest Free Internet:	library – 15-minute walk from hostel
Parking:	parking lot across the street; free parking for private-room guests, $1 discount coupon available for $15 tourist trolley

is this hostel great for you?

SOLO WOMEN Yes. An easy place to make friends over breakfast. Good for rookie hostellers.

PARTY ANIMALS No. The sidewalks roll up around 5pm.

OVER 30 Yes. Interesting sights, nice beach and good shops in this tourist town.

OVER 50 Yes. Elderhostel groups often visit St. Augustine for its historic value.

COUPLES Yes. "Couples rooms" are available & carriage rides through town are very romantic.

FAMILIES Yes. Wonderful hostel for families! Private family room sleeps six & kids under 13 stay free.

GROUPS No. Facility is small and not suitable for large groups.

~ best for partying ~

Hotel Congress
Tuscon, AZ

Santa Barbara Tourist Hostel
Santa Barbara, CA

Ocean Beach International Hostel
San Diego, CA

Elements Hostel
San Francisco, CA

The Tropics
Miami, FL

Blue Moon Guesthouse
Lafayette, LA

The Gershwin Hotel
New York City, NY

Jazz on the Park
New York City, NY

McMenamins Edgefield
Troutdale, OR

Bank Street Hostel
Philadelphia, PA

Georgia Hostels

1 Atlanta
The Atlanta Hostel

Atlanta, Georgia

THE ATLANTA HOSTEL
223 Ponce de Leon
Atlanta, GA 30308
Phone: (404) 875-9449 or
(800) 473-9449
Fax: (404) 872-0042
E-mail: rsup@mindsping.com
Website: www.hostel-atlanta.com

~ what to expect ~

This hostel is smaller – and more interesting – than most city hostels. Instead of a nondescript urban building, the Atlanta Hostel is housed in an old Victorian-style house.

Within this house-turned-hostel is an eclectic mix of furnishings. A beautiful chandelier hangs above a table with plastic chairs. Lace curtains and Civil War photographs adorn the dining room, which also houses a refrigerator. It's a bit unorthodox, but it's not unappealing. In fact, the resulting air of informality is welcome in a hostel.

Guests visiting Atlanta in the summer will be happy to know that the entire hostel, including dorm rooms, is air-conditioned. Dorms have hardwood floors, curtains and closets. The two private rooms are furnished with one queen-size bed, one single bed, chairs, a nightstand, a dresser and a mirror.

Atlanta has all the attractions of a big city and this is a good base from which to explore them.

~ fast facts ~

Dorm Rates:	$17 HOA members, $19 non-members, $18 backpackers/ISIC	**Season:**	all year
Private Rooms:	$42–48 (1) $49–8 (2)	**Office Hours:**	8am–11:45am & 5pm–11:45pm
Credit Cards:	MasterCard & Visa	**Lock-out:**	n/a
Network:	Hostels of America, Backpackers	**Size:**	55 beds
Beds:	spring mattresses		
Kitchen:	small kitchen		
Bathrooms:	house-style baths, a mix of shared & private		
Lockers:	yes		
Extras:	pool table, piano, free coffee and donuts, Internet access		
Be Aware:	Rate discounts apply only to dorm beds.		
In The Area:	Atlanta city attractions		
Local Tip:	Piedmont Park is less than 1 mile away		
Closest Free Internet:	public library		
Parking:	free onsite parking		

is this hostel great for you?

SOLO WOMEN Yes. Safe, quiet and homey.

PARTY ANIMALS No. Fairly quiet hostel.

OVER 30 Yes. Interesting, international crowd.

OVER 50 Yes. Private rooms with attached bathrooms are available.

COUPLES Yes. Private rooms have queen-size beds.

FAMILIES No. Rooms can't sleep more than three people.

GROUPS Yes. Members will have to split up into multiple dorms, though.

~ best for romance ~

Bridge Street Inn
Cambria, CA

HI – Point Montara Lighthouse
Montara, CA

HI – Pigeon Point Lighthouse
Pescadero, CA

HI – Breckenridge (Fireside Inn)
Breckenridge, CO

Pirate Haus
St. Augustine, FL

Circle A Ranch
Cuba, NM

HI – Weisel
Quakertown, PA

Churchill Mansion B&B & Ice House Hostel
Yarmouth, Nova Scotia, Canada

Idaho Hostels

1 Boise
HI – Nampa (Hostel Boise)

Boise, Idaho

HI – NAMPA
(HOSTEL BOISE)
17322 Can-Ada Rd.
Nampa, Idaho 83687
Phone: (208) 467-6858
Fax: (208) 465-5158
E-mail: mail@hostelboise.com
Website: www.hostelboise.com

~ what to expect ~

Few travelers seek out Boise as a vacation destination. And with good reason. There really isn't much going on here. However, cross-country drivers will find it a convenient place to stop as they motor from sea to shining sea.

The owner of this hostel has plenty of experience, having previously owned a B&B and hostel in another location. When she relocated to Nampa, she decided to forgo opening another B&B, preferring the easygoing spirit hostellers embody. She feeds that spirit regularly, often literally, with gifts from her vegetable garden.

Hostel Boise is actually located in a rural area a few miles outside Boise. The facility is basically a 1970s house whose three bedrooms have been outfitted with bunk beds. The décor is dated, but comfortable. The house is spotless and the location is very safe. You'll find more privacy than in a traditional home hostel because the manager lives in a nearby trailer rather than onsite. And given the out-of-the-way location, odds are high that you will be the only guests during your visit.

So, while Boise is no entertainment hub – and Nampa even less so – you'll find a comfortable bed and warm reception at this Middle America home away from home.

~ fast facts ~

Dorm Rates: $15.50 HI members, $18.50 non-members

Private Rooms: $31–35 for 1–2 (one room with a queen-size bunk below and single bunk on top)

Credit Cards: MasterCard & Visa

Network: HI

Beds: spring mattresses

Kitchen: yes

Bathrooms: shared, house-style

Lockers: yes

Extras: free Internet, piano

Be Aware: Bring groceries, as there isn't a store nearby.

In The Area: hiking within1-hour drive of hostel

Local Tip: Bring a book.

Closest Free Internet: onsite

Parking: Free parking at the hostel; call ahead for pick-up from Boise airport ($10) or bus station ($3).

Season: all year

Office Hours: 8am–10:30am & 5pm–10:30 pm

Lock-out: n/a

Size: 13 beds

is this hostel great for you?

SOLO WOMEN Yes. Quiet and safe.

PARTY ANIMALS No. Dull as can be.

OVER 30 Yes. But bring a book.

OVER 50 Yes. With luck, you'll enjoy fresh vegetables from the owner's garden.

COUPLES Maybe. Comfortable, but not romantic.

FAMILIES Yes, but be prepared to entertain yourselves.

GROUPS No. The hostel is relatively small.

~ best for meetings ~

HI – Midpines (Yosemite Bug Hostel)
Midpines, CA

HI – Sacramento (The Mansion)
Sacramento, CA

HI – Crested Butte
Crested Butte, CO

HI – Chicago
Chicago, IL

HI – Boston at Fenway Park (summers only)
Boston, MA

HI – New York City
New York, NY

Laurel Fork Lodge
Hampton, TN

Illinois Hostels

❶ **Chicago**
HI – Chicago
(The J. Ira & Nicki Harris Family Hostel)

Chicago, Illinois

HI – CHICAGO
(THE J. IRA & NICKI HARRIS FAMILY HOSTEL)
24 East Congress Pkwy.
Chicago, IL 60605
Phone: (312) 360-0300
Fax: (312) 360-0313
E-mail: reserve@hichigaco.org
Website: www.hichicago.org

~ what to expect ~

This is one of Hostelling International's newest facilities. Sleeping 500 guests at a time, it's also one of their biggest.

The hostel is situated on several floors of an urban high rise, with the entrance and front desk on the second floor of the building. This unusual but ingenuous layout prevents people from wandering in off the street. It's also just the first of many indications that this hostel takes security very seriously. Each guest receives a key card at check-in. It must be used in the elevator to reach the upper floors, where the bedrooms are located, and to unlock the bedroom door.

The second floor houses all the common areas: the kitchen, dining room, TV room, city information desk and group meeting rooms. The hostel's size makes it especially well-suited for groups, as do the various amenities. The industrial-size kitchen makes it a snap to prepare large meals that can be served in the equally large dining room. Windows cover one full wall of that area, allowing diners to watch people strolling along the streets and riding the L train. The meeting rooms are as modern as you'll find in any corporate building. They vary in size to accommodate small or large sessions and include podiums and presentation resources.

Visitors who come to town on their own will appreciate the assistance the onsite city information desk offers. Staffers are quick to provide information and directions and to answer any and all questions.

Dorm rooms are clean, but unremarkable and fairly large. Larger than I like, in fact. I find that the more people (and backpacks) there are in one room, the messier it can get.

The hostel is located in the museum section of town, near Chicago's world-class Art Institute, the aquarium and planetarium. A free tourist trolley stops at each sight. But most evening hot spots, including those in Bucktown and along Division Street, are quite a ways away. Guests will want to take the subway to reach them. Or even better, pool resources and catch a cab.

~ fast facts ~

Dorm Rates:	$34.50	**Season:**	all year
Private Rooms:	$90–120, seasonal	**Office Hours:**	24 hours
Credit Cards:	MasterCard & Visa	**Lock-out:**	n/a
Network:	HI	**Size:**	500 beds

Beds: spring mattresses

Kitchen: big, new and modern

Bathrooms: shared, dorm-style

Lockers: yes, large ones

Extras: Internet access, city information desk, 2 cafés onsite, pingpong table, TV, group meeting rooms with presentation areas

Be Aware: Dorms are really big; neighborhood can be deserted at night.

In The Area: museums, Art Institute, Navy Pier attractions, lakefront beach

Local Tip: Cafés downstairs have good, cheap food; use the free tourist trolley to visit the museums.

Closest Free Internet: public library

Parking: garage parking nearby for $30/day

is this hostel great for you?

SOLO WOMEN Yes, but find a friend for evening exploration.

PARTY ANIMALS Yes. Grab a cocktail downstairs before heading toward Bucktown.

OVER 30 Yes. Be sure to check out the Art Institute.

OVER 50 Yes. Free tourist trolley available.

COUPLES Not especially. No private rooms.

FAMILIES No. No family rooms.

GROUPS Yes. Especially well-designed for groups.

~ best for mountain biking ~

HI – Crested Butte International Lodge & Hostel
Crested Butte, CO

Leadville Hostel
Leadville, CO

The Rocky Mountain Inn & Hostel
Winter Park/Fraser, CO

High Peaks Hostel
Lake Placid, NY

New Paltz Hostel
New Paltz, NY

Center Street Hostel and Hotel
Moab, UT

Louisiana Hostels

1 Lafayette
Blue Moon Guesthouse

Lafayette, Louisiana

BLUE MOON GUESTHOUSE
215 E. Convent St.
Lafayette, LA
Phone: (337) 234-2422
Fax: (337) 234-2434
E-mail: n/a
Website: www.bluemoonhostel.com

~ what to expect ~

The Blue Moon is my favorite type of hostel – a renovated 100-year-old home with hardwood floors, high ceilings, homey living spaces and lots of local art. The place draws a friendly, grown-up crowd. It'd be easy to show up here for a night and end up staying a week.

But no matter how long or short a stay you anticipate, you need to know about the Blue Moon Saloon. The Saloon is the bar in the back of the hostel. Like any backyard bar, this is a place you'll either love or hate. An awful lot of people love it, making the Blue Moon their sole reason for visiting Lafayette. A different Cajun, folk, blues, jazz or bluegrass band plays till around midnight five nights a week. The Wednesday night Cajun jams are especially popular. The whole town is actually a hotbed of Cajun culture and draws people from around the world. You'll find a significant population of French Canadians who come to dance. Reservations are essential during the annual festivals: Mardi Gras in February and March, Festival International in April and Festivals Acadians in September.

The hostel can host up to 30 guests at one time. Two private rooms are available, one with one double bed, two single beds and an attached bath; the other with one double bed, one single bed and an attached half-bath. Guests may also choose between a coed dorm and a gender-segregated dorm. Dorm rooms sleep 6–12 guests in bunk beds and share private, house-style bathrooms. One of the bathrooms is handicapped-accessible.

The hostel has a pleasant, good-size kitchen for hostellers to use. Other nearby options include the Borden's ice cream parlor next door and the family-run Mediterranean deli across the street. However, everyone who comes to Lafayette should be sure to taste some of the incredible Cajun seafood for which the area is famous. Like Cajun music, this food is hot, spicy and fantastic. The experience is road-trip-worthy.

~ fast facts ~

Dorm Rates: $18–20

Private Rooms: $40–75

Credit Cards: MasterCard, Visa, AMEX

Network: n/a

Beds: spring mattresses

Kitchen: good size

Bathrooms: primarily shared, house-style; one private room with a private bath

Lockers: yes, small ones

Season: all year

Office Hours: 8am–12pm & 5pm–10pm

Lock-out: n/a

Size: 30 beds

Extras: onsite Blue Moon Saloon w/live music, Internet access, laundry, free coffee & tea

Be Aware: The bands will keep you awake till midnight.

In The Area: Cajun music and food, swamp tours, alligator ranch

Local Tip: Guests receive one free drink at the Blue Moon Saloon, art gallery openings second Saturday of each month; bands play downtown Fridays in spring & fall.

Closest Free Internet: public library, just 5 blocks away

Parking: free, onsite parking; limited gated parking available upon request; motorized trolley downtown

is this hostel great for you?

SOLO WOMEN Yes. Most guests here are solo travelers. It's a safe environment where it's easy to make friends.

PARTY ANIMALS Yes. Party out back with a different band each night of the week.

OVER 30 Yes. The crowd here is older than average. You'll not be the only 30-something here.

OVER 50 Yes, if the onsite bar doesn't turn you off.

COUPLES Yes. One "couples room" is available. Come and dance the night away.

FAMILIES No. Bar bands keep guests up till midnight.

GROUPS No. Too small.

"A man travels the world over in search of what he needs, and returns home to find it."

– *George Moore*

Maine Hostels

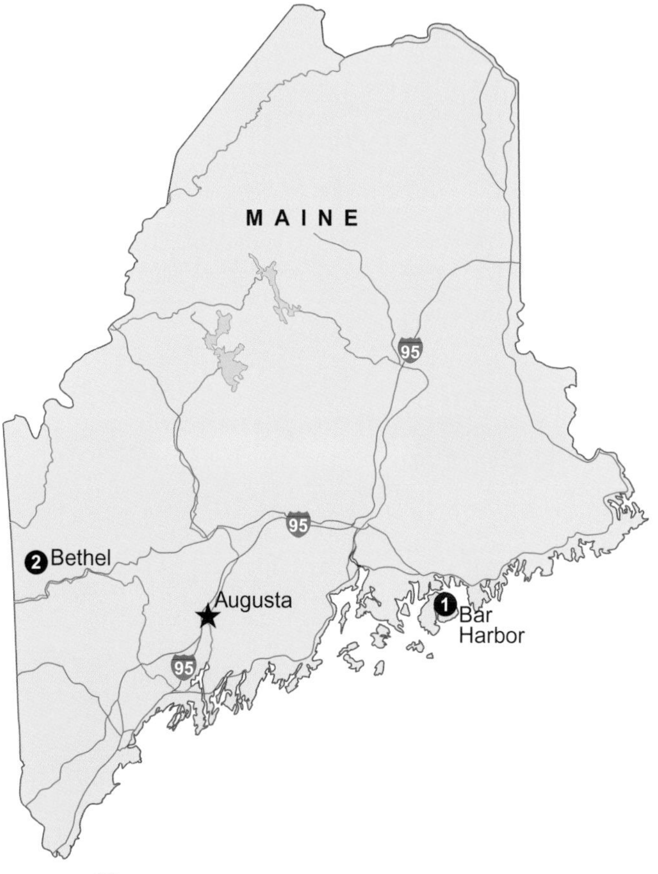

1 Bar Harbor
Mount Desert Island Bar Harbor Hostel

2 Bethel
HI – Bethel (The SnowBoarding House)

Bar Harbor, Maine

MOUNT DESERT ISLAND BAR HARBOR HOSTEL

321 Main St.
P.O. Box 32
Bar Harbor, ME 04609
Phone: (207) 288-5587
Fax: n/a
E-mail: hostelron2003@yahoo.com
Website: www.barharborhostel.com

~ what to expect ~

A visit to Bar Harbor can feel like a pilgrimage.

There are obstacles to overcome. This location isn't especially easy to reach – especially by public transportation. Bar Harbor is way up there, on the edge of the country, practically falling off into Canada. And the brutally cold winter . . . fall . . . and spring . . . make for a pitifully short tourist season. Ah, but the reward wouldn't be nearly as satisfying without having overcome the obstacles.

And rewards do await you. The little town is charming and easy to navigate on foot. Shops, restaurants and bakeries line several streets around the hostel.

The food is also a treat. For a true Maine experience, skip the fancy restaurant and head to one of the rustic dockside cafés where lobsters are served up practically right out of the traps.

You can choose from a host of activities – whale watching, kayaking, even a ferry ride to Canada if you so desire. However, the pièce de résistance is Acadia National Park. Acre for acre, Acadia is my favorite national park. Standing atop the mountains and watching waves crash below is an amazing experience. And pink-and-purple sunsets light up the sky each night. They're guaranteed to make an atheist reconsider his position.

Over a million dollars went into creating the current Bar Harbor Hostel, which opened in July 2004. A decorator was hired to paint the walls in warm pastels and colorful tile and polished hardwood flooring were installed. Antique bookcases donated for the international book swap program are filled with current titles donated by the town library and bookstores.

This hostel houses 32 guests. Most sleep in dorm rooms, but the one private room sleeps up to five people in one queen-size bed, one set of bunk beds and one optional rollaway twin bed. This room has a private half-bath across the hall. All guests share the hall shower rooms, where three showers are available for males and three for female guests.

This hostel is tight on common space, with the pretty dining area serving as the main indoor gathering spot. A table that seats eight is available for guests who use the kitchen or outdoor grill to prepare meals. Weather permitting, guests also congregate outside on the deck.

~ fast facts ~

Dorm Rates: $24, $21 students

Private Rooms: $75 (1 private room)

Credit Cards: MasterCard & Visa

Network: n/a

Beds: spring mattresses

Kitchen: yes

Bathrooms: shared, house-style; private half-bath for private room

Lockers: no

Extras: barbecue grills, deck, movie nights, Internet access, deck

Season: April 15–Nov. 1

Office Hours: 8am–10am & 5pm–8pm

Lock-out: 10am–5pm

Size: 30 beds

Be Aware: Maine doesn't really warm up till July.

In The Area: kayaking, sailing, hiking, biking, whale watching

Local Tip: Sunsets high in Acadia National Park are amazing; 3-minute walk to bus station.

Closest Free Internet: Mount Desert Island library

Parking: free parking onsite; free "Islander" local bus

is this hostel great for you?

SOLO WOMEN Yes. Very safe and pretty.

PARTY ANIMALS Yes, local bars within walking distance.

OVER 30 Yes. Clean, clean, clean.

OVER 50 Yes. Charming community.

COUPLES Yes. Queen-size bed in private room.

FAMILIES Yes. Private room sleeps up to five.

GROUPS Not unless you rent the entire facility.

Bethel, Maine

HI – BETHEL
(THE SNOWBOARDING HOUSE)

646 West Bethel Rd. (Rt. 2)
Bethel, ME 04217
Phone: (207) 824-4224
Fax: (207) 824-8511
E-mail: info@betheloutdooradventure.com
Website: www.hiusa.org

~ what to expect ~

This hostel's surroundings make it worth a visit for anyone with a love for the outdoors.

Hikers have several trail options: the White Mountain Forest, Bethel Recreation Area or perhaps even a segment of the Appalachian Trail. And the skis on the outside of the building are a none-too-subtle hint that skiers and snowboarders will find slopes nearby.

The two-story wood building resembles a number of ski hostels. Which is to say it's comfortable in a thrift store kind of way. The large living room has linoleum floors, country wallpaper and ruffled plaid window valances. The furnishings include an old plaid recliner and coordinating sofas and a small television sits on a corner bookshelf. A long, galley-style kitchen is next door. Twin-bedded bedrooms have comfy spring mattresses. Late risers will appreciate the room-darkening drapes.

The accommodations are basic, but the destination is premium.

~ fast facts ~

Dorm Rates: $19 HI members, $22 non-members

Private Rooms: same as dorm rates

Credit Cards: MasterCard, Visa, Discover, AMEX

Network: HI

Beds: spring mattresses

Kitchen: yes

Bathrooms: shared, house-style

Lockers: no

Extras: free Internet, satellite TV, laundry facilities

Season: May–November

Office Hours: 8am–10am & 5pm–10pm

Lock-out: 10am–5pm

Size: 18 beds

Be Aware: rural atmosphere, no room keys or lockers

In The Area: Bethel Recreational Pathway, White Mountain Forest, Appalachian Trail

Local Tip: just 5 miles to Appalachian Trail

Closest Free Internet: onsite

Parking: free onsite parking

is this hostel great for you?

SOLO WOMEN Yes. Twin beds instead of bunks. No way to lock up, though.

PARTY ANIMALS No. Rural.

OVER 30 Yes. Good proximity to mountain and AT hiking.

OVER 50 Yes. Comfortable beds.

COUPLES No. Twin beds only; definitely not a romantic atmosphere.

FAMILIES Yes. Rooms of various sizes.

GROUPS No. Too small.

"The world is a book, and those who do not travel, read only a page."

– *Saint Augustine*

Maryland Hostels

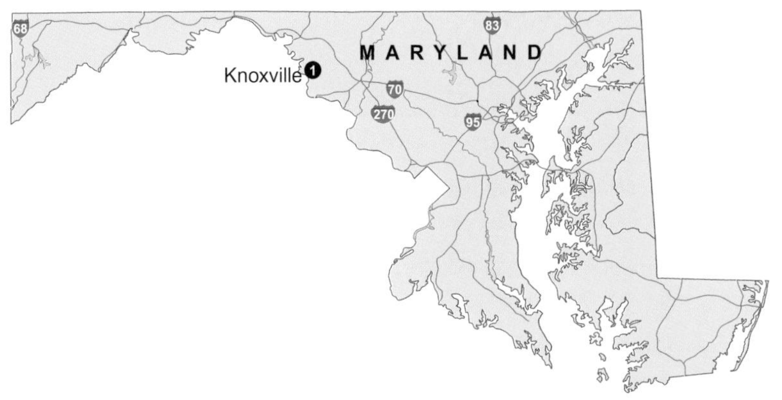

1 Knoxville
HI – Harper's Ferry Lodge

Knoxville, Maryland

HI – HARPER'S FERRY LODGE
19123 Sandy Hook Dr.
Knoxville, MD 21758
Phone: (301) 834-7652
Fax: (301) 834-7652
Website: www.harpersferryhostel.org
E-mail: mail@harpersferryhostel.org

~ what to expect ~

Harper's Ferry is only a short drive from Washington D.C., but hostel guests are more likely to arrive via a hiking trail than an expressway.

From the hostel, a two-mile riverside hike takes you into West Virginia and to the little town of Harper's Ferry; a two-day hike takes you to the city lights of Washington, D.C. And a really, really long hike on the 2,174-mile Appalachian Trail takes you across several states, cities and towns. It's your choice.

If you opt for the quick jaunt into Harper's Ferry, you'll find the town up on a hill above the confluence of two rivers. A bridge across the rivers delivers you to the town park, the spot where walking tours of this historic city originate. If you aren't in the touring mood, you might opt to shop along the hilly cobblestone streets.

If your feet get sore from all the walking, cool them off with a jump in the river. Tourists tend to join organized rafting trips, while locals just rent inner tubes and dive right in. Either alternative is a good way to escape the summer heat and give your feet a rest. A rafting company located directly across from the hostel can help you plan your trip.

The hostel is closed during the day, so guests arrive after 5pm. Dinner can be prepared in the kitchen, which is equipped with two stoves and refrigerators, and eaten in the dining room. Neither is huge, but both are sufficient. The common living space makes the most of every season, with a working fireplace for the winter and an attached deck for warmer weather.

Each of the hostel's two private rooms sleeps six. All other guests sleep in the gender-segregated dorms. Each dorm has six sets of bunk beds – which is more than I like. It's a good bet that one of your 11 sleeping companions will be a snorer. Both dorm guests and those who opt for private rooms share the men's and women's bathrooms located in the dorms.

~ fast facts ~

Dorm Rates:	$17 HI members, $20 non-members; $8.50 under 12
Private Rooms:	$50 for 2; dorm rates for larger groups
Credit Cards:	MasterCard & Visa
Network:	HI
Beds:	spring mattresses
Kitchen:	yes, medium-size
Bathrooms:	shared, dorm-style
Lockers:	no
Extras:	volleyball, badminton, laundry, library of books, fireplace, board games, free coffee, free Internet, $5 pancakes, store, $9/person camping
Season:	mid-March–mid-November
Office Hours:	7am–9am & 6pm–10pm
Lock-out:	9am–6pm
Size:	40 beds
Be Aware:	Private-room guests use the dorm bathrooms; large dorms.
In The Area:	Appalachian Trail hiking, historic town of Harper's Ferry, river rafting
Local Tip:	2-mile hiking trail from hostel to Harper's Ferry
Closest Free Internet:	onsite
Parking:	free onsite parking

is this hostel great for you?

SOLO WOMEN Yes. 75% of guests come from the Appalachian Trail, many of them traveling on their own.

PARTY ANIMALS No. No alcohol allowed in hostel.

OVER 30 Yes. Hostel has a mixed-age clientele.

OVER 50 Yes. Stick to the privates rather than the 12-person dorms, though.

COUPLES Yes. One private room has a double bed.

FAMILIES Yes. Two 6-person family rooms are available.

GROUPS Yes. Hostel can sleep up to 36 people.

"The traveler sees what he sees, the tourist sees what he has come to see."

– *Gilbert K. Chesterton*

Massachusetts Hostels

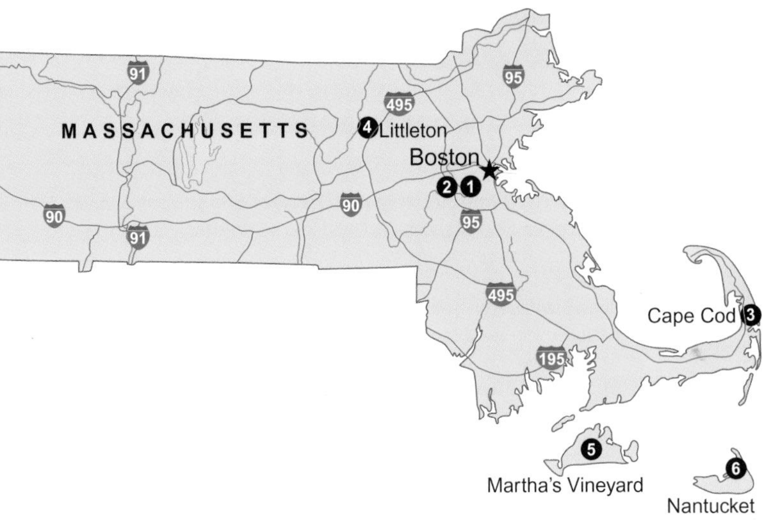

1. **Boston**
   HI – Boston
2. **Boston**
   HI – Boston at Fenway (Summer Hostel)
3. **Cape Code / Eastham**
   Mid-Cape
4. **Littleton**
   HI – Friendly Crossroads
5. **Martha's Vineyard**
   HI – Martha's Vineyard
6. **Nantucket**
   HI – Nantucket

Boston, Massachusetts

HI – BOSTON
12 Hemingway St.
Boston, MA 02115
Phone: (617) 536-9455
Fax: (617) 424-6558
E-mail: bostonhostel@bostonhostel.
Website: www.bostonhostel.org

~ what to expect ~

This is a pretty typical city hostel – a multi-level building that sleeps over 200 people. As with most hostels that play host to so many people, the focus is more on professionalism and less on personal touches. The atmosphere is more pleasant than friendly; the staff is more efficient than social.

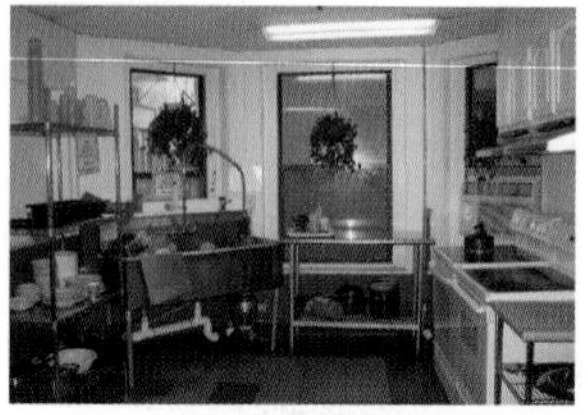

The big advantage this hostel has is its location. The neighborhood is both safe and convenient to popular tourist areas and the management offers free walking tours to help visitors explore the city. It's a solid choice for any tourist.

All common areas are on the first floor. The kitchen is big enough to accommodate small groups. But the dining room, which also serves as the TV room, is filled with long tables that face the screen. Many people prefer to relax in the lobby, which is furnished with a couple of couches, chairs and Internet kiosks.

Each of 10 good-size private rooms sleeps two people, either in twin beds or one set of bunk beds. Other guests stay in gender-segregated dorm rooms that have bunk beds and large lockers. Bathrooms located on each floor are shared by all guests.

~ fast facts ~

Dorm Rates: $32–35 HI members, $35–38 non-members

Private Rooms: $99 (2–4 people)

Credit Cards: MasterCard & Visa

Network: HI

Beds: spring mattresses

Kitchen: yes, medium-size

Bathrooms: shared, dorm-style

Lockers: yes, including extra-large size

Extras: free coffee and donuts, piano, Internet access, ATM machine, free walking tours, meeting room

Be Aware: Despite the high price, the dorms are nothing special.

In The Area: Boston city attractions – museums, clubs

Local Tip: Harvard University (free tour) and The John F. Kennedy Library and Museum ($6–8) are worth seeing and can be reached via the subway system.

Closest Free Internet: public library

Parking: parking lot next door: $15/day, garages $20–25/day

Season: all year

Office Hours: 24 hour

Lock-out: n/a

Size: 246 beds

is this hostel great for you?

SOLO WOMEN Yes. Free walking tours are good opportunities to meet people.

PARTY ANIMALS Yes. No alcohol allowed in the hostel, but good central location.

OVER 30 Yes. Take advantage of the free walking tours.

OVER 50 Yes. Good neighborhood. Boston Pops concerts nearby.

COUPLES Yes. Private rooms sleep two people. Compare prices with those at hotels, though.

FAMILIES No. Too cost-prohibitive for families.

GROUPS Yes. Large hostel with a meeting room.

Boston, Massachusetts

HI – BOSTON AT FENWAY (SUMMER HOSTEL)
575 Commonwealth Ave.
Boston, MA 02115
Phone: (617) 267-8599
Fax: (617) 424-6558
E-mail: fenway@bostonhostel.org
Website: www.bostonhostel.org

~ what to expect ~

Each summer, a Boston University dorm becomes the Boston at Fenway HI hostel. It's a shame this great addition to the city's hostel scene can't be available year 'round.

Whether you prefer a dorm room or a private room, this place has, by far, the best hostel rooms in Boston. The private rooms sleep up to three people in twin beds and have private attached bathrooms. Dorm rooms, furnished with just three twin beds apiece, share bathrooms down the hall. The décor isn't any more interesting than that found in the average student dorm, but all rooms are clean and spacious.

This hostel shines in the bedroom area, but its common areas are a bit lacking. Guests must eat out. Because while there is a large dining room, there isn't a kitchen. And other common rooms are simply underutilized. The eighth-floor room is huge and offers one of the best city views in town. But no one goes there.

As the name suggests, this hostel is located within walking distance of the Fenway Park professional baseball stadium. Visitors are encouraged to attend a game and enjoy this national pastime. This hostel is not as central to other attractions as is the HI facility on Hemingway Street, but Boston is a relatively small city and easy to explore on the subway.

~ fast facts ~

Dorm Rates: $32–37 HI members, $35–40 non-members

Private Rooms: $89 HI members, $92 non-members

Credit Cards: MasterCard & Visa

Network: HI

Beds: spring mattresses

Kitchen: none

Bathrooms: shared, dorm-style for dorms; attached, house-style for private rooms

Lockers: no

Extras: free breakfast, daily activities, Internet access, foosball table

Be Aware: open only during the summer

In The Area: Fenway Park (Red Sox professional baseball) and other Boston city attractions

Local Tip: The original "Cheers" bar doesn't resemble the one in the old TV show.

Closest Free Internet: public library

Parking: some free parking on street, nearby lot $20/24 hours

Season: June 1–August 16

Office Hours: 24 hour

Lock-out: n/a

Size: 300 beds

is this hostel great for you?

SOLO WOMEN Yes. Hostel club outings are a fun and safe way to go out at night.

PARTY ANIMALS Maybe. The hostel isn't an alcohol-friendly facility, but Boston is very much an alcohol-friendly city. Be sure to check out an Irish pub or two.

OVER 30 Yes. Drivers will appreciate the street parking.

OVER 50 Yes. Best rooms of the two recommended Boston hostels.

COUPLES Yes. After dark, check out the romantic view from the 8th floor.

FAMILIES Not unless they are small. Private rooms sleep only three people.

GROUPS Yes. Convenient location for taking in a baseball game. No kitchen, though.

Cape Cod / Eastham, Massachusetts

HI – MID-CAPE
75 Goody Hallet Dr.
Eastham, MA
Phone: (508) 255-2785
Fax: (508) 240-5598
E-mail: midcapehostel@yahoo.com
Website: www.capecodhostels.org

~ what to expect ~

This unassuming hostel, tucked away in a quiet section of the Cape, sits in contrast to the wealth found elsewhere on the island.

The hostel grounds include a series of small wood buildings and a flower garden. A kitchen and dining area occupy most of the main building. Furniture in the small sitting room includes a couple of rocking chairs and a matching futon.

Separate buildings house the men's and women's dorms. Each building has eight built-in wood bunk beds; free linens are provided for the plastic-covered mattresses. The shared bathrooms are located in the main building, which can be inconvenient in the middle of the night.

Livelier sections of the Cape, including the Sandwich beaches and P-town shops, are nearby for those with transportation. A car or bicycle is definitely an asset on this island. Those who choose a bicycle will want to check out the 30-mile "rail trail" bike path.

~ fast facts ~

Dorm Rates:	$24 HI members, $27 non-members	**Season:**	mid-May–mid-September
Private Rooms:	n/a	**Office Hours:**	7am–10am & 4pm–10pm
Credit Cards:	MasterCard & Visa	**Lock-out:**	n/a
Network:	HI	**Size:**	48 beds
Beds:	spring-mattresses, covered in plastic		
Kitchen:	yes		
Bathrooms:	shared, dorm-style in main building		
Lockers:	no		
Extras:	free linens		
Be Aware:	Bring a car or bike to travel to sights.		
In The Area:	beaches, shopping		
Local Tip:	Cape Cod Rail Trail (30-mile bike path)		
Closest Free Internet:	unknown		
Parking:	free onsite parking, "Orleans" bus stop		

is this hostel great for you?

SOLO WOMEN Yes. Safe area, but can be really quiet.

PARTY ANIMALS No. Alcohol is banned and nothing is nearby.

OVER 30 Yes. Mellow vibe.

OVER 50 Maybe, but the bathroom location can be annoying.

COUPLES No. No private rooms.

FAMILIES Maybe. Best if you rent an entire dorm.

GROUPS Yes. Common areas can accommodate small groups.

Littleton, Massachusetts

HI – FRIENDLY CROSSROADS
247 Littleton County Rd.
P.O. Box 2266
Littleton, MA 01460
Phone: (978) 456-9386
Fax: (978) 456-9386
E-mail: info@friendlycrossways.com
Website: www.hiusa.org

~ what to expect ~

Most of this hostel's current clientele is composed of groups who come out for a quiet retreat. It's well-suited for that, but individual travelers will also find it to be a nice place for a quiet getaway weekend.

Henry David Thoreau's famous Walden Pond is nearby. Truthfully, the pond itself isn't any more interesting than any other pond. However, in the right mindset, a visit to the cabin where Thoreau lived and wrote can be a powerful experience.

You'll find the quaint, comfortable hostel a nice place to return and relax after you've made that worthwhile pilgrimage. Hardwood floors, lace curtains and homemade quilts abound. But don't expect to find a television. Even black-and-white reception would mess with the contemplative vibe.

Groups fit well into this hostel, and size has a lot to do with that. The two-stove kitchen is relatively large. There is plenty of seating in the dining room, and dorm rooms sleep up to 22 people. (Although one small room sleeps just three.) Guests in dorms sleep in twin beds and bunks. Unless you want a pseudo-camping experience though, you might want to avoid the room that has a couple of mattresses on the floor.

Guests who seek more privacy can opt for a private room. Some are furnished with just one twin bed for an individual traveler.

If you're tired of the city lights – or can no longer afford Boston's $40 rates – come spend a couple of days here. You'll leave rested and refreshed.

~ fast facts ~

Dorm Rates:	$15 HI members, $18 non-members	**Season:**	year-round
Private Rooms:	$20 HI members, $23 non-members	**Office Hours:**	8am–10am & 5pm–10pm
Credit Cards:	no	**Lock-out:**	10am–5pm
Network:	HI	**Size:**	48 beds
Beds:	spring mattresses		
Kitchen:	yes		
Bathrooms:	shared, house-style		
Lockers:	no		
Extras:	piano, free sheets, free coffee and tea, computer plug-in access		
Be Aware:	no lockers or locks on doors		
In The Area:	Walden Pond		
Local Tip:	Mass transit runs from Littleton to Boston.		
Closest Free Internet:	Littleton public library		
Parking:	free onsite parking		

is this hostel great for you?

SOLO WOMEN Yes. Come for a quiet weekend away.

PARTY ANIMALS No. Way too quiet.

OVER 30 Yes. Request a dorm with fewer beds if you want a quieter stay.

OVER 50 Yes. Those driving may find this a cheaper, more relaxing base from which to explore Boston.

COUPLES Yes. Quaint, comfy rooms can be romantic.

FAMILIES Yes. Space is available, although kids might not find it exciting.

GROUPS Yes. Groups often rent the entire place for meetings and retreats.

Martha's Vineyard, Massachusetts

HI – MARTHA'S VINEYARD
Edgartown-West Tisbury Rd.
P.O. Box 3158
West Tisbury, MA 02575
Phone: (508) 693-2665 or
(888) 901-2087
Fax: n/a
E-mail: mvhostel@yahoo.com
Website: www.usahostels.org

~ what to expect ~

Martha's Vineyard is a fun place to escape from everyday life. Visitors leave their cares – and their cars – behind on the mainland as they step aboard the ferry that carries them away. Most visitors will be bunking in extremely expensive B&Bs and guesthouses. It's great that Hostelling International has made it possible for the rest of us to play alongside them.

The island has a couple of picture-postcard villages full of expensive shops and gingerbread cottages. Probably the best way to see it all is to buy a one-day bus pass and ride around for a few hours. After taking in the bus overview, you can hop off at your favorite stop and spend the rest of the day sightseeing on foot.

The hostel, located in a rural area apart from the main villages, is best reached by bus or bicycle. The house sleeps up to 75 people and is especially well-suited for groups. Be sure to call ahead to find out if any groups have reservations for the days you plan to visit. The Girl Scout troops tend to take control of the place when they're in residence.

Spacious segregated and coed dorms sleep 20+ people in bunk beds. In the common room, you'll find an eclectic mix of furniture and a fireplace in lieu of a television. It's management's way of encouraging guests to stop watching other people's lives for a few days – and actively participate in their own.

~ fast facts ~

Dorm Rates: $18–26

Private Rooms: $96 (1–4 people)

Credit Cards: MasterCard & Visa

Network: HI

Beds: spring mattresses (covered in plastic)

Kitchen: large and spacious

Bathrooms: newer; shared, dorm-style

Lockers: yes, large ones on the front porch

Extras: volleyball court, Internet access, free linens and towels, pingpong table, $1.50 pancakes

Season: April 11–October 13

Office Hours: 8am–10am & 4pm–10pm

Lock-out: 10am–4pm

Size: 74 beds

Be Aware: A cup of coffee will cost you 50¢.

In The Area: shops, historic gingerbread cottages, bike rides

Local Tip: Buy a $5 bus pass instead of the $18 bus tour.

Closest Free Internet: public library

Parking: Cars are prohibitively expensive and not common.

is this hostel great for you?

SOLO WOMEN Yes. A good, inexpensive way to experience the island.

PARTY ANIMALS Not especially.

OVER 30 Yes. Avoid the July Girl Scout troop invasion, though.

OVER 50 No. Too crowded.

COUPLES Yes. Can sleep in coed dorms.

FAMILIES Yes. One family room available.

GROUPS Yes. An optimal hostel for groups.

Nantucket, Massachusetts

HI – NANTUCKET
31 Western Ave.
Nantucket, MA 02554
Phone: (508) 228-0433
Fax: (508) 228-5672
E-mail: nantuckethotel@yahoo.com
Website: www.usahostels.org

~ what to expect ~

Notorious as a summer home for the rich and famous, Nantucket is an island most regular folks have to experience as a day trip. Fun can be had, but it must be cut short in order to catch the last ferry out. Hotel and B&B rooms are simply too expensive.

Smart regular folks have another option, though. Relax and take another sip of your drink as the ferry leaves the dock, secure in the knowledge that you've got a bunk reserved at this hostel.

The hostel is a two-story A-frame building whose wood exterior is echoed in hardwood floors and ceilings in the downstairs common rooms. The dining room is furnished with long, school-cafeteria-style tables with attached plastic seats and an old upright piano. The living room is more refined, with matching furniture and floral window valances.

The large dorm rooms are separated for men and women. The clean and airy women's dorm is housed upstairs in an oversize attic. The room can get pretty noisy, given the number of people who share it. Shared bathrooms start the day clean, but can get messy after 20 people use them to get ready for the morning.

This hostel is well-suited for smaller groups of any sort, and school groups often use it in the summer. But there aren't any private rooms here. So chaperones must be prepared to sleep in the same dorms as their charges.

Groups and individuals will find Nantucket a picturesque, low-key island. Shopping is a prime activity for some visitors. But since most boutiques are quite expensive, window-shopping, peoplewatching and sunbathing provide cost-free alternatives.

~ fast facts ~

Dorm Rates: $18–26

Private Rooms: n/a

Credit Cards: MasterCard & Visa

Network: HI

Beds: spring mattresses (covered in plastic)

Kitchen: large for the size of the hostel

Bathrooms: shared dorm-style

Lockers: yes, small ones

Extras: piano

Be Aware: Bathrooms are messy in the morning after 20 people use them.

Season: late April–mid-October

Office Hours: 8am–10am & 4pm–10pm

Lock-out: 10am–4pm

Size: 49 beds

In The Area: beach only 2 blocks away; town, 3 miles away

Local Tip: Some bus routes are seasonal – be sure to check.

Closest Free Internet: public library

Parking: Cars are prohibitively expensive. Everyone uses the bus.

is this hostel great for you?

SOLO WOMEN Yes. Relaxing island.

PARTY ANIMALS Yes. Better since the curfew was abolished.

OVER 30 Yes. You won't find a cheaper way to hobnob with the folks of Nantucket.

OVER 50 No. Smallest bedroom sleeps 11 people; limited bathroom privacy.

COUPLES Yes. You can stay in the coed dorm.

FAMILIES No. No private rooms.

GROUPS Yes. Probably most suitable for groups.

"Journeys, like artists, are born and not made. A thousand differing circumstances contribute to them, few of them willed or determined by the will — whatever we may think."

– *Lawrence Durrell*

Montana Hostels

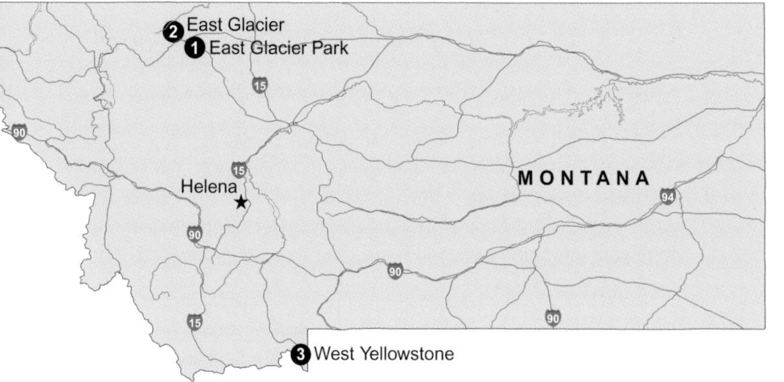

1. **East Glacier Park**
   Backpacker's Inn
2. **East Glacier**
   HI – East Glacier (Brownie's)
3. **West Yellowstone**
   Madison Hotel, Gift Shop & Hostel

East Glacier Park, Montana

BACKPACKER'S INN
29 Dawson Ave.
Box 94
East Glacier Park, MT 59434
Phone: (406) 226-9392
Fax: n/a
E-mail: n/a
Website: n/a

~ what to expect ~

The best thing about the Backpacker's Inn is its price: $10 a night is hard to beat.

The second best thing is its location. It's in the middle of town, across from the Amtrak station and next door to the most popular Mexican restaurant in East Glacier.

The hostel itself is essentially a set of cabins behind the restaurant. A stone pathway leads guests through the shared back yard and to the cabin. The picnic table under the trees and the back deck off the restaurant are the closest this hostel comes to common rooms.

The hostel is an interesting design contradiction. Along the exterior, plants bloom in flower beds and boxes. But the interior walls are unfinished pressed particleboard. The dorms are also extremely minimalist. You'll find them clean, but without any furniture other than a couple sets of wood bunk beds and, perhaps, a chair. This hostel seems to have been designed for folks just looking for an inexpensive place to lay their heads at night. Two upgraded private cabins with private bathrooms are also available.

If you're torn between camping and hostelling, this could be the spot for you. Hot showers, a bed off the ground and a price that can't be beat. Plan to explore the park during the day and visit the restaurant for dinner and drinks at night. You'll have a fine time here.

~ fast facts ~

Dorm Rates: $10

Private Rooms: varies

Credit Cards: MasterCard, Visa, & AMEX

Network: n/a

Beds: spring mattresses in privates, foam mattresses in dorms

Kitchen: no

Bathrooms: shared, dorm-style in dorms; private in private rooms

Lockers: no

Extras: picnic table

Be Aware: simple; no common rooms

In The Area: Glacier National Park hiking

Local Tip: The attached Mexican restaurant, Serrano's, is the town hot spot.

Closest Free Internet: unknown

Parking: free onsite parking; across the street from Amtrak station

Season: May 1 – Oct. 1

Office Hours: call ahead

Lock-out: n/a

Size: 10 beds

is this hostel great for you?

SOLO WOMEN Yes. Amtrak travelers will appreciate the location.

PARTY ANIMALS Yes. Grab a Margarita at Serrano's.

OVER 30 Maybe. Good alternative to camping.

OVER 50 Maybe. Probably better off at Brownie's.

COUPLES Not especially.

FAMILIES No. You're better off at Brownie's.

GROUPS Not especially. No common rooms or kitchen.

East Glacier, Montana

HI – EAST GLACIER (BROWNIE'S)
1020 Highway 49, Box 229
East Glacier, MT 59434
Phone: (406) 226-4426
Fax: n/a
E-mail: browniesegp@yahoo.com
Website: n/a

~ what to expect ~

Brownie's Grocery and Hostel is a self-described "rustic, historic log building which houses a grocery store and deli on the main floor, and a hostel on the second floor." It's an accurate description of a combination that actually works pretty well.

The small country store is about the size of a gas station convenience store. But it has all the basics, plus a deli, bakery and computer with Internet access.

Log walls create a wood-cabin atmosphere upstairs in the hostel. A small common room at the top of the staircase is outfitted with a couple of old overstuffed rockers, some fuzzy orange benches and a few books and board games. The kitchen next door is comparably simple: A table and some folding chairs constitute its dining area. Walk down the hall in either direction to find the bedrooms. The dorms are basic. But the private rooms – accessorized with quilts, lamps and antique furniture – are nicer than those at most hostels. Bathrooms have stall showers and bathtubs. An upstairs covered balcony spans the front of the house and effectively doubles the size of the common space. Guests can sit up there and watch people come and go along the main street into town. Free parking is available onsite and the Amtrak station is within walking distance.

Most people are here to visit Glacier National Park. Famed for its Big Sky sunsets and wild animal life, the park is a treat even for seasoned National Park visitors. A local bus makes regular daily trips into the park during tourist season, so those traveling by public transportation needn't miss out on the fun.

~ fast facts ~

Dorm Rates: $13 HI members, $16 non-members

Season: May 15–October 1 (weather permitting)

Private Rooms: $18 for 1 HI member, $21 for 1 non-member, $23 for 2 HI members, $26 for 2 non-members, $38 for 4 HI members, $41 for 4 non-members

Office Hours: 7am–9pm

Lock-out: n/a

Size: 36 beds

Credit Cards: MasterCard, Visa, Discover

Network: HI

Beds: spring mattresses

Kitchen: yes

Bathrooms: shared, dorm-style

Lockers: yes, in dorms

Extras: Internet access, laundry, bike storage, grocery, deli, bakery

Be Aware: No late night check-in; extreme snow may delay May opening.

In The Area: Glacier National Park, hiking, bike rental, golf, swimming, horseback riding, Museum of Plains Indians

Local Tip: Shuttle available into Glacier National Park.

Closest Free Internet: n/a

Parking: free onsite parking; 6 blocks from Amtrak station

is this hostel great for you?

SOLO WOMEN Yes. Super-safe.

PARTY ANIMALS No. Not happenin' at all.

OVER 30 Yes. More character than a budget motel.

OVER 50 Yes. Private rooms will offer an especially comfortable night's sleep.

COUPLES Yes. Private room with double bed available.

FAMILIES Yes. Up to four can sleep in larger private room.

GROUPS No. Too small.

West Yellowstone, Montana

MADISON HOTEL, GIFT SHOP & HOSTEL

139 Yellowstone Ave.
Box 1370
West Yellowstone, MT 59758
Phone: (406) 646-7745 or
(800) 838-7745
Fax: (406) 646-9766
E-mail: MadisonHotel@wyellowstone.com
Website: www.wyellowstone.com/madisonhotel

~ what to expect ~

Montana hostels all seem to do double duty. Hostel-grocery stores. Hostel-restaurants. Or, like this one, a hostel-gift shop-hotel. It's not a bad idea. The sister business always seems to be beneficial to hostellers and generally lends the hostel more character than it might otherwise have.

Built in 1912, the Madison began life as a hotel for summer tourists. The pine log building's historic atmosphere was carefully retained when the old-fashioned gift shop opened in 1959.

The hostel is located on the second floor of the building. The first floor is divided into the gift shop and a lobby decorated in Early American Hunting Lodge. The furniture is made of carved pine logs. A bear skin, deer antlers and mounted bison adorn the walls. When the gift shop closes at night, hostellers have exclusive use of this room's fireplace, small television and VCR and Internet–accessible computer.

The hostel bedrooms, bathrooms and shower rooms are located upstairs. Dorms are furnished with antique sinks and mirrored dressing tables; each of the dorm rooms sleeps three people in one set of bunk beds and one twin bed. Private rooms vary in size and sleep up to four people. Some share bathrooms with dorm guests, while others have private baths. Quilts and linens are already on all of the beds, waiting for guests' arrival. The Madison also offers motel rooms, but they don't have the hostel's Old Yellowstone ambiance.

The town of West Yellowstone is located, not surprisingly, just west of Yellowstone National Park. The park is home to "Old Faithful" and more other active geysers than any place in the world. Tourists will enjoy the other hydrothermal attractions (mud pots, hot springs and fumaroles) and the canyon along Yellowstone River. This is a large park with a lot to see. It's best to reserve a couple of days to explore it all.

~ fast facts ~

Dorm Rates: $22 HI members, $24 non-members

Private Rooms: $29 (1 twin), $39–49 (1 double), $55 (2 doubles)

Credit Cards: MasterCard, Visa, Discover, AMEX

Network: n/a

Beds: spring mattresses

Kitchen: no

Bathrooms: shared, house-style; some private rooms with private bath

Lockers: no

Extras: Linens & towels are provided, TV & VCR, Internet access.

Be Aware: All rooms are non-smoking.

In The Area: Yellowstone National Park, hiking

Local Tip: city bus to Bozeman on Tuesdays & Thursdays

Closest Free Internet: public library next door

Parking: free onsite parking

Season: May 25–mid-October

Office Hours: 8am–10pm

Lock-out: n/a

Size: 16 beds

is this hostel great for you?

SOLO WOMEN Yes. Private rooms for one person are a good deal.

PARTY ANIMALS No. Quiet hostel in a quiet town.

OVER 30 Yes. Old Yellowstone atmosphere will get you ready for the park.

OVER 50 Yes. Private shower rooms.

COUPLES Yes. Private rooms with double beds are available.

FAMILIES Yes. Larger private rooms will sleep four.

GROUPS Maybe. Small, no kitchen or dining room.

"Like all great travellers, I have seen more than I remember, and remember more than I have seen."

– Benjamin Disraeli

New Hampshire Hostels

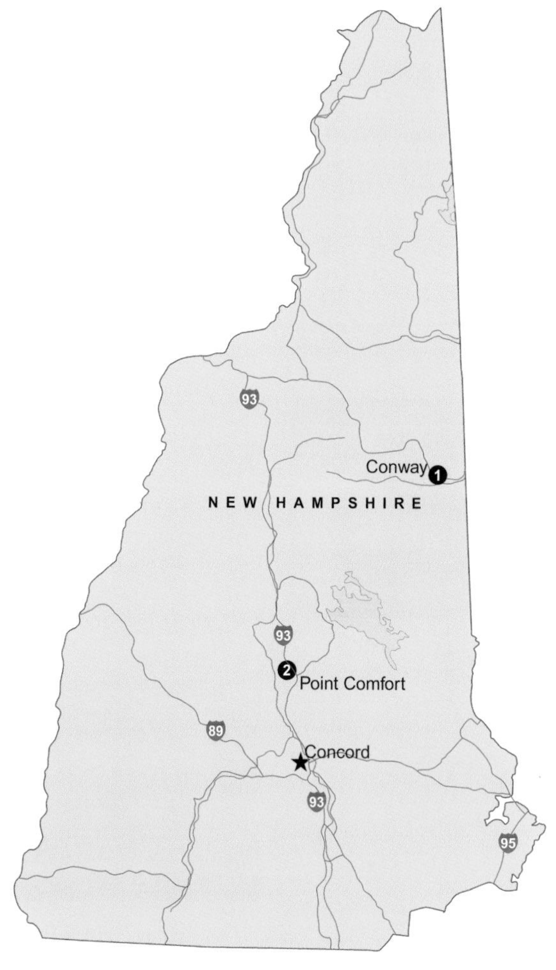

1 Conway
HI – White Mountains
(Albert B. Lester Memorial Hostel)

2 Sanbornton
Shaker Woods Farm at Point Comfort

Conway, New Hampshire

HI – WHITE MOUNTAINS (ALBERT B. LESTER MEMORIAL HOSTEL)
36 Washington St.
Conway, NH 03818
Phone: (603) 447-1001
Fax: (432) 339-6758
E-mail: conwayhostel@yahoo.com
Website: www.conwayhostel.com

~ what to expect ~

This is one of the best places to take novice hostellers. Newbies apprehensive about what they'll find at a hostel will immediately be put at ease here.

To locate the hostel, just look for a two-story white house with blue shutters. You'll need to look carefully, though. Except for the HI sign, the hostel blends right in with the other houses in its residential neighborhood.

The same homey atmosphere permeates the hostel interior. Floral curtains and hanging baskets decorate sun-filled windows in a cozy living room at the front of the house. Furniture includes matching sofas with accent pillows, and folks are welcome to sit and watch a small television or grab one of the old novels or travel books from the shelf. Other common areas include a dining room and a well-appointed kitchen.

Guests can choose to sleep in either a dorm or a private room. Bedrooms have hardwood floors, curtains and floral wallpaper. Private rooms also have side tables and reading lamps. Everyone shares the bathrooms down the hall.

Most people who stay in Conway use the town as a base from which to explore the White Mountains. The area bustles with activity all year 'round. Warmer months bring hikers, bikers and rock climbers; colder months bring skiers and ice climbers.

~ fast facts ~

Dorm Rates: $21 HI members
$24 non-members
$10 kids 13 and under

Private Rooms: $48 for 2 adults and up to 3 children

Credit Cards: MasterCard & Visa

Network: HI

Beds: spring mattresses

Kitchen: yes

Bathrooms: shared, dorm-style

Lockers: yes

Extras: free linens

Be Aware: Paper plates & plastic utensils are not allowed due to commitment to recycling.

Season: all year

Office Hours: 7:30am–10am & 5pm–10pm

Lock-out: 10am–2pm

Size: 48 beds

In The Area: White Mountain hiking, climbing, biking, skiing, ice climbing, kayaking and antique shops

Local Tip: Don't come to see the Old Man of the Mountain: The legendary stone face fell off the mountain in 2003!

Closest Free Internet: public library, 1 block away

Parking: free onsite parking

is this hostel great for you?

SOLO WOMEN Yes. Especially if you're an outdoorswoman.

PARTY ANIMALS No. Not a real party town or hostel.

OVER 30 Yes. Mixed-age crowd here.

OVER 50 Yes. An eclectic area – antiques in town and hiking in the park.

COUPLES Yes. Cozy private rooms.

FAMILIES Yes. The family room is a good value.

GROUPS Yes. Good place for hiking/climbing clubs.

Sanbornton, New Hampshire

SHAKER WOODS FARM AT POINT COMFORT
30 Lower Smith Rd.
Sanbornton, NH 03269
Phone: (603) 528-1990 phone
E-mail: info@shakerwoodsfarm.com
Website: http://shakerwoodsfarm.com

~ what to expect ~

Shaker Woods has no dorm rooms, whose availability is one of the criteria for Sedobe-recommended hostels. So, it shouldn't, technically speaking, be included in this guidebook. But Eva and Jack offer such a unique experience, I just had to make an exception to the rule.

They've invested a fair bit of time, energy and resources into converting the horse barn into a guesthouse of sorts. One-time horse stalls are now bedrooms, but you needn't worry about any leftover hay between the sheets or feed in the corner. All traces of the animals who once occupied these spaces are long gone, but the building has retained its barn structure: Sliding open the stall door to enter your room is fun and imparts a childlike sense of adventure. Each room in the barn sleeps one or two people in one double bed or two twin beds. The drapes that replace one wall in each of these rooms are pretty, but they aren't soundproof. Those requiring privacy – and having more money – may opt for one of the traditional house bedrooms upstairs.

The common room and kitchenette are also upstairs. Decorated like an enclosed front porch and accented with lace curtains and quilts, the common room is very homey. The kitchenette is equipped with a small refrigerator, toaster oven and electric tea kettle – appliances best suited for heating beverages and making snacks. Not much more is needed, however, since a free breakfast is available each morning

Shaker Woods isn't really a hostel, so it shouldn't be included. But it's a place hostellers will love. So it is.

~ fast facts ~

Dorm Rates: n/as

Private Rooms: $30 for 1 person, $50 for 2, $80–115 for B&B rooms

Credit Cards: MasterCard, Visa, Discover

Network: n/a

Beds: spring mattresses

Kitchen: microwave, refrigerator and toaster oven only

Bathrooms: shared house-style in barn; attached in others

Lockers: no

Extras: free breakfast, farm products on sale

Be Aware: serious cancellation policy; smoke-free facility; several poodles onsite

In The Area: farmers market, lakes, Shaker villages, mountains within a 1-hour drive

Local Tip: tax-free factory outlet stores just 6 miles away; flagship L.L.Bean store only 2 hours away

Closest Free Internet: wireless router onsite

Parking: free onsite parking

Season: all year

Office Hours: 8am–10pm

Lock-out: n/a

Size: 5 beds

is this hostel great for you?

SOLO WOMEN Yes, if you can afford the $30 price for one person.

PARTY ANIMALS No. Quiet environment.

OVER 30 Yes. Nearby Shaker villages make for an interesting trip.

OVER 50 Yes. Guests will find a common room and breakfast typical of a B&B.

COUPLES Yes. One of the barn rooms has a double bed.

FAMILIES Yes. Kids can watch Eva milk the goats in the morning.

GROUPS No. Too small.

"Wandering re-establishes the original harmony which once existed between man and the universe."

– *Anatole France*

New Mexico Hostels

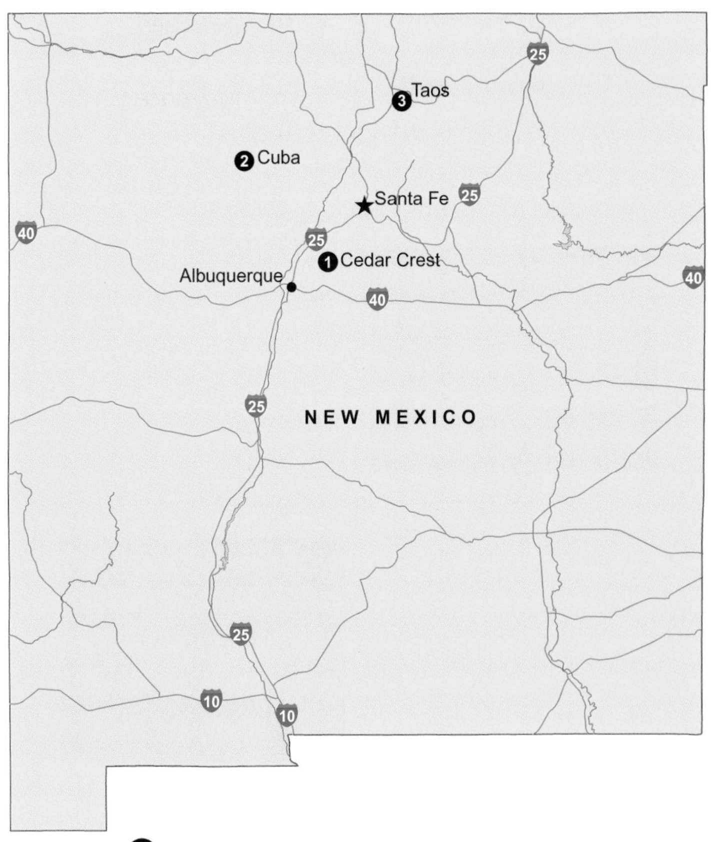

1 Cedar Crest
Sandia Mountain Hostel

2 Cuba
Circle A Ranch

3 Taos
HI – Taos (The Abominable Snowmansion)

Cedar Crest, New Mexico

SANDIA MOUNTAIN HOSTEL
12234 Highway 14 North
Cedar Crest, NM 87008
Phone: (505) 281-4117
Fax: n/a
E-mail: info@newmexicohostels.com
Website: www.newmexicohostels.com

~ what to expect ~

Constructed of pine walls, log support beams and tiled floors, this rustic Southwestern hostel blends right into its desert setting.

The oversized cabin has four main rooms: a kitchen, a common room and two dorm rooms. The kitchen isn't huge, but it's sufficient for the size of the hostel. A wood-burning stove and protective brick wall dominate the common room in the center of the house.

The dorm rooms have high ceilings, and big windows line the top of the walls. Down below, up to 10 guests sleep in extra-tall bunk beds. Those in the bottom bunks will appreciate the extra headroom with which the beds were built.

Special features of this hostel include an outdoor shower and a sauna with a rainwater plunge bath. And there are donkeys that kids can ride.

The hostel is located on The Turquoise Trail, a scenic byway punctuated by a host of jewelry shops. Those shops aren't likely to offer the best deals. But they do offer some of the best handmade jewelry in the area.

~ fast facts ~

Dorm Rates:	$14	**Season:**	year-round
Private Rooms:	$20–60	**Office Hours:**	4:30pm–10pm
Credit Cards:	MasterCard & Visa	**Lock-out:**	n/a
Network:	n/a	**Size:**	20 beds

Beds: spring mattresses

Kitchen: yes

Bathrooms: shared, dorm-style

Lockers: yes

Extras: sauna with cold rainwater plunge bath, outdoor showers, camping, linen rentals, group rates available, private rooms in separate building with kitchen, bath and wood-burning stove

Be Aware: pretty sleepy area

In The Area: Native American jewelry and gift shops (area known as the "Turquoise Trail"), hiking, skiing

Local Tip: Resident donkeys give trail rides.

Closest Free Internet: Tijeras public library

Parking: free onsite parking

is this hostel great for you?

SOLO WOMEN Maybe. Good shopping for turquoise jewelry nearby, but can be dead quiet.

PARTY ANIMALS No. Really quiet.

OVER 30 Yes. Preferable to Santa Fe hostel.

OVER 50 Yes. Mellow setting.

COUPLES Yes. Private rooms available.

FAMILIES Yes. Kids can ride the donkeys.

GROUPS Yes, if renting the entire facility.

Cuba, New Mexico

CIRCLE A RANCH
Box 2142
Cuba, NM 87013
Phone: (505) 289-3350
Fax: n/a
E-mail: n/a
Website: www.circlearanch.info

~ what to expect ~

Built in the 1920s as a hunting lodge, this New Mexico ranch has a long and interesting history.

The current family of owners turned it into a summer camp where generations of little girls played and rode horses. In time, the girls grew up and the owners grew older and less inclined to manage such an involved program. Younger family members now operate the ranch as a hostel for part of each year.

Located near the San Pedro Wilderness Area, the ranch encompasses over 300 acres of forested land, giant old trees, swimming holes and hiking trails. Most of the nearby Native American pueblos are open to the public.

The hostel itself is an old two-story adobe hacienda. An outdoor walkway along the veranda connects a number of upstairs bedrooms. All four private rooms have double beds. One has a private bath; the other three share three bathrooms with the dorm guests. Two large dorm rooms sleep 22 in bunk beds.

Books are scattered about, as if to encourage guests to pick one up. I liked doing my reading on the veranda. Others may choose to head downstairs and curl up on comfy couches next to the stone fireplace in the big open living room.

Fresh eggs are for sale in the well-stocked kitchen next door to the living room. The adjacent dining area is furnished with long wood tables and benches. In the warmer months, guests can also dine outside on the patio.

This big rambling house can get pretty quiet. You're not going to find a rockin' party when you arrive here. However, it's perfect for someone seeking a tranquil retreat, a couple looking for a romantic getaway or a family seeking a wholesome reunion setting.

~ fast facts ~

Dorm Rates:	$20	**Season:**	May–mid-October
Private Rooms:	$45–55	**Office Hours:**	vary: call ahead.
Credit Cards:	MasterCard & Visa	**Lock-out:**	n/a
Network:	n/a	**Size:**	26 beds

Beds: spring mattresses in privates, foam mattresses in dorms

Kitchen: yes

Bathrooms: shared, dorm-style; one private room with private bath

Lockers: no

Extras: camping permitted for groups ($20)

Be Aware: Wild animals have been seen on hiking trails.

In The Area: Native American pueblos; Chaco Culture National Historical Park is 50 miles west.

Local Tip: Pueblo ceremonial dances are generally open to the public, but photography isn't allowed.

Closest Free Internet: Cuba public library (1 hour/day)

Parking: free onsite parking

is this hostel great for you?

SOLO WOMEN Yes. Very safe (but you may not have anyone to talk to).

PARTY ANIMALS No. You'll die of boredom.

OVER 30 Yes. Peaceful retreat atmosphere.

OVER 50 Yes. Check out nearby Chaco Canyon and Native American pueblos.

COUPLES Yes. Good getaway spot to de-stress.

FAMILIES Yes. Popular for family reunions.

GROUPS Yes. Lots of room.

Taos, New Mexico

HI – TAOS
THE ABOMINABLE SNOWMANSION
INTERNATIONAL HOSTEL & SKI LODGE
P.O. Box 3271
Taos, NM 87571
Phone: (505) 776-8298
Fax: (505) 776-2107
E-mail: snowman@newmex.com
Website: www.snowmansion.com

~ what to expect ~

This hostel is the site of one of my favorite hostel memories – the evening that evolved into an impromptu concert in the round. On a road trip to celebrate a birthday, a couple of roots musicians from Boulder, Colorado ended up at the Snowmansion. They broke out their instruments, someone else grabbed his guitar and the rest of us added our voices to the mix. Our makeshift band played and sang our way through an evening of folk and bluegrass standards. It was a blast!

I can't guarantee that you'll have the same experience, but you just never know. This hostel has many different personalities – depending on the season you visit and where you choose to stay. The ski season will make for a busier hostel; the summer is more relaxed. The main building is pretty typical, but there are also tents in the back yard for adventurous sleepers.

The pink adobe exterior of the main building gives way to an interior that is more eclectic than Native American. On the first floor, you'll find a small kitchen, some dorm rooms and the main common area that fills most of the building. Comfortable chairs and banquettes surround an enclosed fire pit and a piano and pool table occupy the other side of the room. The second floor includes private rooms, a reading area and an Internet station.

The simple dorm rooms have attached bathrooms and sleep about 10 guests at a time. A family-size private room is furnished with one double bed and three sets of bunk beds.

This facility features a daytime lock-out, but those with no place to go can hang out in the separate building out back. It's got a small kitchen and living room, but be prepared for a pretty rustic environment.

One last note: A sign at the front desk reads: "No weirdos. No non-bathers. We reserve the right to refuse service to anyone." You just *gotta* love that.

~ fast facts ~

Dorm Rates: $15–22, vary by season

Private Rooms: $28–52

Credit Cards: MasterCard, Visa & Discover

Network: HI

Beds: spring mattresses

Kitchen: yes

Bathrooms: house-style

Lockers: no

Extras: free coffee, pool table, piano, indoor fire pit, Internet access, cooked breakfast during ski season

Season: all year

Office Hours: 8am–noon & 4pm–10pm

Lock-out: n/a

Size: 60 beds

Be Aware: Hostel is actually 9 miles outside of Taos; summer tent camping allowed in the back yard; no laundry.

In The Area: Taos art community, skiing, hiking, rafting

Local Tip: Quiet summer season is a nice time to visit.

Closest Free Internet: Taos

Parking: street parking; shuttles available from Albuquerque and Santa Fe

is this hostel great for you?

SOLO WOMEN Yes. Be sure to check out the Taos art galleries.

PARTY ANIMALS No. No alcohol allowed in hostel and no bars nearby.

OVER 30 Yes. The dorms will be cozy in the winter, though.

OVER 50 Yes, in the summer.

COUPLES Yes. Private rooms available.

FAMILIES Yes. Family room available – summer will be quieter than ski season.

GROUPS Yes. Ask about group rates and catered dinners.

"If you reject the food, ignore the customs, fear the religion and avoid the people, you might better stay home."

– James Michener

New York Hostels

❶ **Cape Vincent**
HI – Tibbetts Point Lighthouse

❷ **Lake Placid**
High Peaks Hostel

❸ **New Paltz**
New Paltz Hostel

❹ **New York City**
Central Park Hostel

❺ **New York City**
Chelsea Star Hotel

❻ **New York City**
The Gershwin Hotel

❼ **New York City**
HI – New York City

❽ **New York City**
Jazz On the Park

Cape Vincent, New York

HI – TIBBETTS POINT LIGHTHOUSE
33439 County Route 6
Cape Vincent, NY 13618-3174
Phone: (315) 654-3450
Fax: n/a
E-mail: lighthousehostel@tds.net
Website: www.hiusa.org

~ what to expect ~

Tibbetts Point is the only lighthouse hostel on the East Coast.

Like its two California counterparts, the hostel isn't actually in the lighthouse. The base of the building has been turned into a small museum dedicated to the history of the lighthouse. The still-active light housed in the top of the building casts its beam across the waters each evening, creating a brilliant show for guests.

The building next door is home to the hostel. It's easy to see that the draw to Tibbetts Point is the lighthouse, not the simple accommodations. A step inside feels like a step back in time. Dark paneling and dated wallpaper cover the walls; linoleum and brown shag carpet cover the floors. With two tables and chairs to seat 10, the kitchen serves as the main common room. The dorm's tall wood bunk beds have comfortable spring mattresses.

The hostel facility may not be something special, but the location truly is. The Point is right on the water, with inspiring views wherever you look. Unlike the California lighthouses high up on cliffs, this one is at sea level. Sitting in one of the Adirondack chairs, listening to the waves, you get a real sense of oneness with the water and those who've sailed past in years gone by.

~ fast facts ~

Dorm Rates:	$14 HI members $17 non-members
Private Rooms:	same
Credit Cards:	MasterCard & Visa
Network:	HI
Beds:	spring mattresses
Kitchen:	yes
Bathrooms:	shared, house-style
Lockers:	no
Extras:	board games, TV, linen rental
Be Aware:	no heat or air conditioning
In The Area:	lighthouse museum, beaches
Local Tip:	French festival 2nd week of July
Closest Free Internet:	Cape Vincent public library
Parking:	free onsite parking
Season:	mid-May–late October
Office Hours:	7am–9:30am & 5pm–10pm
Lock-out:	9:30am–5pm
Size:	26 beds

is this hostel great for you?

SOLO WOMEN Yes, if looking for a quiet getaway.

PARTY ANIMALS No. No party action here.

OVER 30 Yes. Unique location.

OVER 50 Yes, especially nautical types.

COUPLES Yes. Evening light show can be romantic.

FAMILIES Not especially. Smaller common areas.

GROUPS Not especially, unless lighthouse fanatics.

Lake Placid, New York

HIGH PEAKS HOSTEL
5956 Sentinel Rd.
Lake Placid, NY 12946
Phone: (518) 523-4951
Fax: n/a
E-mail: info@highpeakshostel.com
Website: www.highpeakshostel.com

~ what to expect ~

Home to an Olympic training facility, Lake Placid attracts outdoorsmen – and women – year 'round. This intimate hostel sleeps 25 and is located just a few miles from the bobsled and luge rides open to anyone with a sense of adventure. As a matter of fact, this contemporary facility is close to everything in town.

Free linens and towels are provided to guests in both of the private rooms as well as those in the dorms. And guests are invited to enjoy a free breakfast that includes homemade treats. After much cajoling, frequent guests persuaded the owner to post the most popular recipes on the Website. So you can enjoy a taste of High Peaks even when you can't be there in person.

Lake Placid winters are frigid, but a wood-burning stove provides welcome warmth for hostel guests. In the summer, Lake Placid visitors keep active by hiking nearby mountains or playing in the town lake. Swimmers can walk into the water from a lakeside beach and boaters can choose between a canoe and a paddleboat. The quaint little downtown will entice you to shop along its streets.

If you happen to be in town for the Fourth of July, you'll be in for a treat. The celebration begins with a parade whose highlights are local celebrities in convertibles and the high school marching band. After the parade has passed by and the sun's gone down, fireworks release showers of color above the lake. People take their blankets and lawn chairs to the water's edge to listen to the band and marvel at the spectacle. This is small-town America at its finest.

~ fast facts ~

Dorm Rates: $22.20, tax included

Private Rooms: $55, tax included

Credit Cards: no

Network: n/a

Beds: futon & spring mattresses

Kitchen: yes

Bathrooms: shared

Lockers: no

Extras: free linens & towels, free breakfast, TV, VCR, laundry, Internet access ($2/day), wood-burning stove

Be Aware: Winters are really cold.

In The Area: hiking, swimming, boating (paddleboats, canoes), shopping

Local Tip: public bobsled and luge rides at the Olympic Training Center in town; stellar Fourth of July fireworks over the lake

Closest Free Internet: town library

Parking: free onsite parking

Season: all year

Office Hours: 8:00am–10:00am & 4:00pm–10:00pm

Lock-out: 10:00am–4:00pm

Size: 25, including 2 private rooms

is this hostel great for you?

SOLO WOMEN Yes. Friendly little hostel and town.

PARTY ANIMALS Not especially.

OVER 30 Yes. Good hiking nearby.

OVER 50 Yes. Fantastic home-made breakfasts.

COUPLES Yes. Private rooms available.

FAMILIES Maybe. Good family town.

GROUPS No. Too small.

New Paltz, New York

NEW PALTZ HOSTEL
145 Main St.
New Paltz, NY 12561
Phone: (845) 255-6676 or
(845) 505-7252 (cellular)
Fax: n/a
E-mail: newpaltzhostel@yahoo.com
Website: www.newpaltzhostel.com

~ what to expect ~

"Shared accommodations for those looking for an open and thoughtful experience while on their travels" reads the sign on the wall. It's a lovely sentiment echoed throughout the hostel.

The small two-story home houses a living room, a kitchen, one men's dorm, one women's dorm and two private rooms. Hardwood floors, colorful wall murals, Bob Marley posters and a big polka dot teddy bear give the rooms a warm, fun atmosphere conducive to socializing. Guests relax on modern couches and chairs while chatting in the cozy little living room and visit in the kitchen while whipping up breakfast and dinner.

Each of the private rooms has one set of bunks plus one twin bed. The dorm rooms are furnished with bunk beds. There's a bathroom across the hall from the men's dorm, which sleeps six. Another bathroom is attached to the women's dorm, which sleeps four.

When the hostel closes for the afternoon, most guests head out to the Shawangunks Mountain Range (locally referred to as "the gunks") for some world-class climbing and hiking. Those who aren't up for such a workout can tour the local wineries or walk through town to the campus of SUNY at New Paltz.

Whatever you do, get out, have some fun and bring back a story or two. As the owners note, "The point is to learn from others something new, or a new way of seeing things, to experience new thoughts and ideas and to contribute to your own experience, as well as the experiences of your fellow guests." Again, a lovely sentiment.

~ fast facts ~

Dorm Rates: $25

Private Rooms: $63–88 (1–2 people)

Credit Cards: MasterCard & Visa

Network: n/a

Beds: spring mattresses

Kitchen: yes

Bathrooms: mix of shared & attached, house-style

Lockers: no

Extras: laundry, BBQ grill, gardens & koi pond, free linens & towels, free local phone, free use of bicycles, free Internet

Be Aware: maximum stay: 2 weeks

In The Area: world-class rock climbing, hiking, cross country skiing, mountain biking, rail trail, wineries, historic stone homes

Local Tip: lots of free food in the kitchen (eggs, milk, etc.)

Closest Free Internet: onsite

Parking: free onsite parking, near bus station

Season: all year, but must call ahead & make a reservation December 15–April 15 (same-day reservations OK)

Office Hours: 4pm–midnight

Lock-out: 10am–4pm; no lock-out for private rooms

Size: 18 beds

is this hostel great for you?

SOLO WOMEN Yes. Friendly atmosphere.

PARTY ANIMALS No. Alcohol-free hostel and quiet, small town.

OVER 30 Yes. Hikers and climbers will love the area.

OVER 50 Yes. Nice front porch for summer socializing.

COUPLES Maybe. Two private rooms available, but they have twin beds.

FAMILIES Maybe. Private rooms sleep just three people; larger families can rent the entire hostel.

GROUPS No. Too small.

New York, New York

CENTRAL PARK HOSTEL
19 West 103rd St.
New York, NY 10016
Phone: (212) 678-0491
Fax: n/a
E-mail: n/a
Website: www.centralparkhostel.com

~ what to expect ~

New York City hostels are unique. You'll find fancy onsite bars and cafés, yet bedrooms tend to be tiny and kitchens and TV rooms rare. An exception to that rule, the Central Park Hostel is as close to a traditional hostel as you'll find in the Big Apple.

Other than HI-New York, this is the only recommended hostel in town that has a kitchen. The room is small, but those overwhelmed by the high costs of everything in the city will appreciate the opportunity to cook their own meals. Even those who plan to sample the city's vast array of restaurants will appreciate being able to store leftovers in the refrigerator. The Central Park also has lockers and a TV room.

Both dorm rooms and private rooms are available as sleeping accommodations and all share one-person bathrooms. The third sleeping option is to rent a studio apartment with a private bath. The apartments aren't cheap, but they're a good value in Manhattan.

The Central Park may not have the glitz of some of the other Manhattan hostels, but it has more of the practical features that many hostellers have come to depend on.

~ fast facts ~

Dorm Rates: $25–30

Private Rooms: $75 (1–2 people); studio apartments with private bath $99–129

Season: all year

Office Hours: 24 hours

Lock-out: n/a

Size: 250 beds

Credit Cards: MasterCard & Visa

Network: n/a

Beds: spring mattresses

Kitchen: yes, small

Bathrooms: shared, house-style in all but studio apts.

Lockers: yes

Extras: Internet access, TV, foosball table

Be Aware: Central Park is dangerous at night.

In The Area: New York City attractions

Local Tip: Subway lines B&C run nearby. (B is an express.)

Closest Free Internet: public library

Parking: some street parking

is this hostel great for you?

SOLO WOMEN Yes. Friendly vibe.

PARTY ANIMALS Maybe. No HI rules here.

OVER 30 Yes. Good for long-haul travelers wanting to cook their own meals.

OVER 50 Yes. Private room options.

COUPLES Yes. "Couple rooms" available.

FAMILIES Yes. Studio apartments available.

GROUPS Maybe. Size is OK, but no group meeting rooms are available.

New York, New York

CHELSEA STAR HOTEL
300 West 30th St.
New York, 10001
Phone: (212) 244-7827
Fax: (212) 279-9018
Website: www.starhotelny.com
E-mail: reservations@starhotelny.com

~ what to expect ~

Don't be turned off by the bright blue door and painted awning that make up the Chelsea Star's entrance. Not being able to see inside the building can be a bit daunting, but don't worry. The minimalist exterior isn't unusual in Manhattan, and the lack of windows is due to the hostel's location on the building's second floor.

After the front desk buzzes you through the locked front door, you climb a set of stairs to reach the hostel. Once there, you'll feel reassured right away. The front desk area and hallways are painted a warm, bright gold and accented with silver light fixtures. The floor has a metallic silver covering, and the combination creates an atmosphere that's cool and modern, yet intimate.

The same atmosphere suffuses the private rooms, where this hostel shines. These spaces aren't huge, but they are well-appointed. The walls are painted festive colors, and traditional hardwood furniture is juxtaposed with contemporary

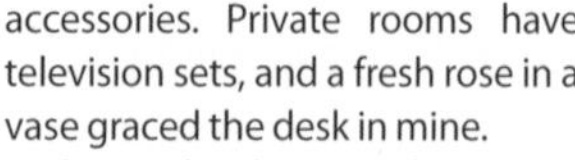

accessories. Private rooms have television sets, and a fresh rose in a vase graced the desk in mine.

Those who don't opt for private rooms will find the dorms to be fairly standard. Noise from the terrace outside the window can be annoying, but the rooms do have nice attached bathrooms.

There isn't a kitchen or any common area other than the terrace, so people don't tend to spend a lot of time socializing here. The Chelsea Star is a good choice for anyone. However, it's probably best suited for couples – or anyone else who has traveling companions with whom to pass the time and share the cost of a private room.

~ fast facts ~

Dorm Rates:	$25.50–$29	**Season:**	all year
Private Rooms:	$79–$109	**Office Hours:**	24 hours
Credit Cards:	MasterCard & Visa	**Lock-out:**	n/a
Network:	n/a	**Size:**	60 beds
Beds:	spring mattresses		
Kitchen:	no		
Bathrooms:	attached		
Lockers:	yes		
Extras:	free linens, patio with picnic tables		
Be Aware:	Courtyard next to dorm can get noisy at night.		
In The Area:	New York City attractions		
Local Tip:	only a 3-hour drive to/from Boston		
Closest Free Internet:	public library		
Parking:	garage parking $25/day, 1 block from Penn Station (train station and subway stop)		

is this hostel great for you?

SOLO WOMEN Maybe. Good neighborhood and nice facility, but not a great place to meet people. I'd choose one of the other ones first.

PARTY ANIMALS Not especially. The Gershwin Hotel or Jazz on the Park are better choices, since they have onsite drinking establishments.

OVER 30 Yes. Modern, private rooms and convenient location.

OVER 50 Yes, if staying in a private room. Too noisy otherwise.

COUPLES Yes. Overall, probably the best NYC hostel for you.

FAMILIES Not especially. Small hostel without a kitchen.

GROUPS No. Too small.

New York, New York

THE GERSHWIN HOTEL
7 East 27th St.
New York, NY 10016
Phone: (212) 545-8000
Fax: (212) 684-5546
E-mail: reservations@gershwinhotel.com
Website: www.gershwinhotel.com

~ what to expect ~

Late nights. Cool clubs. Hot models. If this is what you're hoping to find in New York City, head on over to The Gershwin Hotel.

The hostel is just one small part of the Gershwin business. Most of the building is dedicated to hotel rooms, which are nice but rather pricey. The hostel dorm rooms aren't anything special, but a much lower price tag is attached. Part of the reason these clean, basic rooms appear so stark is their contrast to the rest of the hotel.

Modern art decorates the exterior as well as the interior of The Gershwin. The giant opaque horns that jut out from the front of the building are certainly memorable. And once you step off the city sidewalk and into the building, you'll immediately be struck by the hot pink artwork and streamlined furniture. This ain't your father's hostel. It's fun and hip and makes guests feel as if *they* are just a little more fun and hip. The fact that the hostel clientele includes more struggling models than international travelers enhances that sensation.

To keep things interesting for these trendy guests, the hotel brings in entertainment several times a week. It might be live music one night, a controversial off-Broadway production the next. You never know what you'll find. Even those who choose to sleep elsewhere would be advised to check out the evening festivities.

The hostel has a breakfast café, but no kitchen; a concierge and dry cleaning service, but no TV room. This isn't the most practical choice of accommodations, but it's likely to be the most fun.

~ fast facts ~

Dorm Rates:	$33–56	**Season:**	all year
Private Rooms:	$99–170	**Office Hours:**	24 hours
Credit Cards:	MasterCard & Visa	**Lock-out:**	n/a
Network:	n/a	**Size:**	24 beds

Beds: spring mattresses

Kitchen: no

Bathrooms: attached, house-style

Lockers: no

Extras: breakfast café, entertainment 3 times per week – music, off-Broadway productions &/or comedy acts; meeting rooms, concierge, Internet access, rooftop terrace, fax, dry cleaning service

Be Aware: plain dorms, expensive privates

In The Area: New York City attractions

Local Tip: This is actually a cool, hip nightspot.

Closest Free Internet: public library

Parking: garage parking $25/day

is this hostel great for you?

SOLO WOMEN Yes. Dress to impress at night and no one need know you're staying in the budget rooms.

PARTY ANIMALS Yes. This is the place to be!

OVER 30 Yes. A sophisticated good time.

OVER 50 Not especially. The trendy crowd tends to be fairly young.

COUPLES No. No hostel private rooms; hotel rooms are expensive.

FAMILIES No. Not a family vibe.

GROUPS Maybe. Large enough to accommodate groups; meeting rooms are available.

New York, New York

HI – NEW YORK CITY
891 Amsterdam Ave.
New York, NY 10025
Phone: (212) 932-2300
Fax: (212) 662-6731
E-mail: reservations@hinewyork.org
Website: www.hinewyork.org

~ what to expect ~

One of HI's largest, this professional, efficient hostel offers some of the best lodging values in the city. Especially for solo travelers and large groups. Each year, thousands of guests stay here while they tour the East Side, West Side, all around the town.

A concierge is available to help those traveling on their own. Maps are provided; city tours can be arranged. Other handy services include free walking tours, a café and a small gift shop that sells souvenirs, calling cards and subway MetroCards.

During my last visit, a Girl Scout troop and a group of Latin American teenagers were staying at the hostel, whose facilities often attract groups. The three rooms available for meetings and events range in size and hold 25–120 attendees. Tables, chairs and audio-visual equipment can be rented from the hostel.

The kitchen isn't very big. But there is plenty of room to eat there as well as in a large downstairs indoor dining room and an outdoor courtyard outfitted with picnic tables. Several good restaurants are within walking distance.

Those too tired to go out in the evenings will find that the hostel affords quite a few diversions: television, Play Station and X-Box games and free movies. Those who do venture out will appreciate the hostel's safe neighborhood and manned 24-hour security desk.

Each of the two private family rooms has one queen-size bed and one set of bunk beds. One room has a private bath; the other shares a hall bath with occupants of the dorm rooms. The dorms are clean. But furnished with little other than bunk beds and lockers, they lack personality. Bathrooms have small dressing areas that provide additional privacy.

The clientele at this hostel is quite diverse. Guests include people of all ages, traveling alone and in groups, on business and on vacation. This hostel may not have a lot of character, but it offers outstanding value and meets the needs of many New York City visitors.

~ fast facts ~

Dorm Rates:	$29–38; $16.50 for children 14 and under	**Season:**	all year
Private Rooms:	$120–135	**Office Hours:**	24 hours
Credit Cards:	MasterCard, Visa, Discover & AMEX	**Lock-out:**	n/a
Network:	HI	**Size:**	615 beds
Beds:	spring mattresses, covered in plastic		
Kitchen:	yes, large		
Bathrooms:	shared, dorm-style		
Lockers:	yes		
Extras:	breakfast café, concierge, Internet access, patio, Play Station games, free linens & towels, laundry, pool table, chapel and group meeting rooms		
Be Aware:	large, plain dorms		
In The Area:	New York City attractions		
Local Tip:	restaurants on Broadway and Amsterdam		
Closest Free Internet:	public library		
Parking:	free street parking at night, daytime meter parking		

is this hostel great for you?

SOLO WOMEN Yes. Join a walking tour to meet people.

PARTY ANIMALS Maybe. OK as a base, but no alcohol in hostel and not located in a party scene.

OVER 30 Yes. Check out the restaurants on Amsterdam and Broadway.

OVER 50 Yes. Mixed crowd here. Elevators to all floors.

COUPLES No. No private rooms for couples.

FAMILIES Maybe. Family rooms that sleep four are available, but a bargain hotel may be a better value.

GROUPS Yes. Multiple meeting rooms are available for events.

New York, New York

JAZZ ON THE PARK
36 W. 106th St.
New York, NY 10025-3805
Phone: (212) 932-1600
Fax: (212) 932-1700
E-mail: info@jazzonthe park.com
Website: www.jazzonthepark.com

~ what to expect ~

Not surprisingly, Jazz on the Park is located just off Central Park and has a jazz club in the basement.

Central Park is the only green space of any size in this city of glass, steel and concrete. Residents use it to escape the stress of urban life, and it's always filled with joggers, dog-walkers and intramural sports teams. Visit when you need a break from the city sights. Be aware though, that the park is very safe during the day, but very dangerous after dark.

At night, hostellers can hop on the subway and head to clubs or restaurants in any part of the city. Or guests may choose to simply stay "home" on nights when the hostel's club is open. The basement space, redone in an industrial silver theme, is outfitted with a bar and a pool table.

During the day, guests can hang out in the upstairs café. With exposed brick walls and a modern, less-industrial décor, the café is a sunny, comfortable place. A free breakfast is provided each morning and other items are sold throughout the day.

It's clear that hostel management has chosen to spend its financial resources on the common areas. The club and café are well done. Despite comfortable spring mattresses on the metal bunks, the bedrooms could best be described as institutional.

Conveniently located and equipped with fun common areas and onsite entertainment, this hostel offers more than most. It's a good choice for travelers who intend to be out socializing and sightseeing rather than staying in their rooms.

~ fast facts ~

Dorm Rates:	$23 and up
Private Rooms:	$57 for 1 person, $85 for 2 people
Credit Cards:	MasterCard & Visa
Network:	n/a
Beds:	spring mattresses
Kitchen:	no
Bathrooms:	shared, dorm-style
Lockers:	yes, coin-operated
Extras:	jazz club/bar downstairs, café, free breakfast, Internet access, pool table, TV, free linens, laundry
Be Aware:	mattresses covered in plastic
In The Area:	New York City attractions
Local Tip:	yummy French Caribbean restaurant nearby
Closest Free Internet:	public library
Parking:	lot parking $10/day, $17 Super Shuttle bus from airport

Season:	all year
Office Hours:	24 hours
Lock-out:	n/a
Size:	280 beds

is this hostel great for you?

SOLO WOMEN Yes. Social atmosphere.

PARTY ANIMALS Yes. Bar located in basement makes for convenient partying.

OVER 30 Yes. Dorm rooms are too small, but that keeps them pretty quiet.

OVER 50 Not especially.

COUPLES Yes. Private rooms available.

FAMILIES No. Not a family vibe.

GROUPS Maybe. Adequate size, but no meeting facilities.

"Through travel I first became aware of the outside world; it was through travel that I found my own introspective way into becoming a part of it."

– *Eudora Welty*

Oregon Hostels

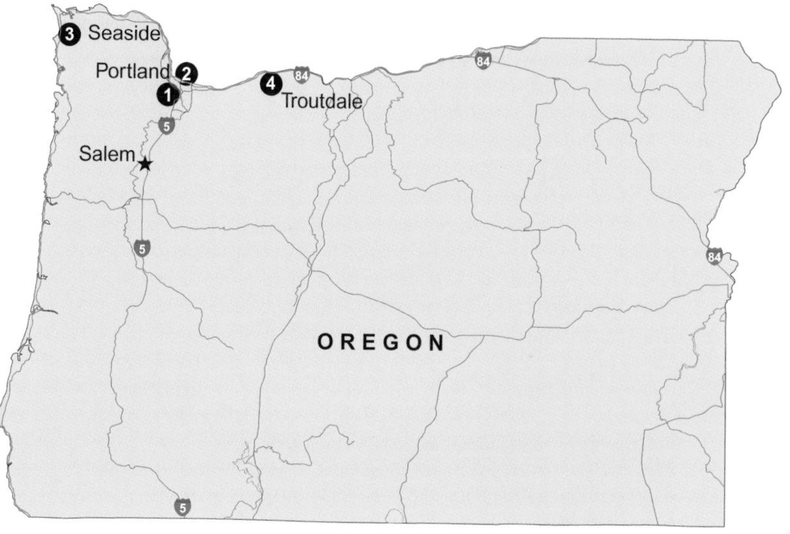

1 Portland
HI – Hawthorne District

2 Portland
HI – Portland Northwest

3 Seaside
HI – Seaside

4 Troutdale
McMenamins Edgefield

Portland, Oregon

HI – HAWTHORNE DISTRICT
3031 SE Hawthorne Blvd.
Portland, OR 97214
Phone: (503) 236-3380
Fax: (503) 236-7940
E-mail: hip@portlandhostel.org
Website: www.portlandhostel.org

~ what to expect ~

Portland has two good hostels. The better one for your stay depends largely on which neighborhood you prefer.

Think of Portland as a family. The Northwest neighborhood is the successful older sister who has moved uptown. The Hawthorne District is the fun-loving younger brother who lives in a house with six other guys, all doing whatever they can to avoid getting real jobs.

Red, orange and lavender walls give the interior of this hostel a fun, friendly vibe. The first floor has an open floor plan and the front desk sits behind the small common room. It opens into a dining room whose wood table and benches seat 8–10 people. A doorway leads from the dining room into a kitchen that's adequate, but unspectacular.

A bathroom, shower room and women's dorm are also located on the first floor. There are additional bathrooms upstairs, as well as private rooms and the men's dorm. Tent campers occupy the back yard whenever the weather permits.

The hostel itself reflects the laid-back character of the neighborhood. Like HI-Northwest, this hostel is a refurbished old house that's not especially big. Unlike that facility, however, Hawthorne has a wide front porch that effectively doubles the amount of common space. And management has no problem with guests and guitars moving out onto the porch at night when things indoors must quiet down.

You needn't worry that management's casual approach might compromise cleanliness: Everything here is scrubbed every day. But you shouldn't assume that the laid-back attitude applies to drinking. This hostel is part of the Hostelling International Network, which means no alcohol is allowed inside. But that just gives you one more reason to explore the neighborhood.

~ fast facts ~

Dorm Rates: $13–16 HI members
$16–19 non-members

Private Rooms: $38

Credit Cards: MasterCard, Visa, Discover & JCB

Network: HI

Beds: mix of foam & spring mattresses

Kitchen: yes

Bathrooms: house-style

Lockers: yes

Extras: Internet access, laundry, tent camping in summer

Be Aware: Dorm rooms are pretty big.

In The Area: world's largest used bookstore (Powell's), skate park, art museum, Rose Garden, Japanese Gardens, Saturday market, weekly art gallery fair

Local Tip: Powell's Books has a store in Hawthorne. The downtown location is near a great CD shop where you can listen to any new or used CD in stock.

Closest Free Internet: Internet café 10 blocks away or public library (1hour/day)

Parking: free street parking

Season: all year

Office Hours: 8am–11pm

Lock-out: n/a

Size: 50 beds

is this hostel great for you?

SOLO WOMEN Yes. Welcoming, chatty crowd.

PARTY ANIMALS Yes. Several casual bars & brew pubs in the area.

OVER 30 Yes. Not too quiet, not too rowdy.

OVER 50 Yes. Especially if you're an old hippie. ☺

COUPLES Yes, private rooms are available.

FAMILIES No. Not really a kid vibe.

GROUPS No. Too small.

Portland, Oregon

HI – PORTLAND NORTHWEST
1818 NW Gilsan St.
Portland, OR 97209
Phone: (503) 241-2783
Fax: (503) 525-5910
E-mail: hinwp@teleport.com
Website: www.2oregonhostels.com

~ what to expect ~

Not too big, not too small, full of diverse neighborhoods, easy to explore on foot: Portland is a city designed for hostellers.

The Northwest neighborhood is one of Portland's best. Eclectic shops and restaurants share the streets here with beautiful stone cathedrals and restored old homes. In order to secure this location, however, the hostel owner obviously had to compromise on size. Guests will find that space is at a premium.

The sunny dining room, which doubles as the common room, is really the only place for people to mingle. It's here that maps are unfolded and recommendations are traded as guests plan their days. Posters that cover the walls are gold mines of staff recommendations on restaurants, bars, worthwhile sights and inexpensive fun.

A tourist's itinerary is likely to include the city's renowned rose garden, museums, market and skate park. However, some hostellers never venture beyond Powell's Books, the world's largest used bookstore.

When choosing a bed for the night, savvy travelers will opt for a private room at this hostel. Multiple dorm rooms are separated only by curtains, so your risk of getting a snoring roommate is pretty high. There is talk of expansion, however, so that may soon change. Inquire when you make a reservation.

Note: When visiting downtown Portland, you'll find a disproportionate number of people living on the street and in the parks. You'll also find that they aren't typical of homeless people found in cities throughout the United States. For some reason, Portland seems to attract young people who choose to live on the street as some sort of "social experiment." They don't walk around muttering to themselves, don't appear to be dangerous and sometimes don't even ask for money. Most are actually quite friendly. It's just a strange and sad situation.

~ fast facts ~

Dorm Rates: $16–19 HI members; $19–non-members

Private Rooms: $30–42 off-season; $43–59 peak season

Credit Cards: MasterCard, Visa, Discover & JCB

Network: n/a

Beds: foam mattresses

Kitchen: yes, small

Bathrooms: house-style

Season: all year

Office Hours: 8am–11pm

Lock-out: n/a

Size: 35 beds

Lockers: yes, small ones in bedrooms

Extras: Internet access, wireless Internet access, linen/towel rental, laundry, free local calls, free bagels

Be Aware: No locks on individual rooms; basement storage is not very secure.

In The Area: world's largest used bookstore (Powell's), Art Museum, Pearl District shopping, Rose Garden, Japanese Gardens, Saturday art fair

Local Tip: Mission Theater brewpub-theatre for beer, food and $3 movies; free downtown buses and trolleys; huge, tasty burritos from Pioneer Square

Closest Free Internet: public library (1 hour/day)

Parking: street parking pass available for $5 deposit

is this hostel great for you?

SOLO WOMEN Yes. Nice, safe neighborhood.

PARTY ANIMALS Yes. An assortment of bars can be found in the Pearl District.

OVER 30 Yes. Don't miss Powell's Books.

OVER 50 Yes. A convenient free bus line runs downtown.

COUPLES Yes, but reserve well in advance for a private room.

FAMILIES Yes. Family rooms are available.

GROUPS No. Too small.

Seaside, Oregon

HI – SEASIDE
930 N. Holladay Dr.
Seaside, OR 97138
Phone: (503) 738-7911
Fax: (503) 717-0163
E-mail: seaside@teleport.com
Website: www.2oregonhostels.com/seaside

~ what to expect ~

A memorable vacation doesn't necessarily involve fancy architecture and wild nightlife. This hostel is located in an old motel building. It isn't anything special to look at, and it would be a mistake to expect to find a martini bar nearby.

However, the town of Seaside and its more sophisticated neighbor, Cannon Beach, offer plenty for those who appreciate the simple pleasures found along the Pacific coast.

The Oregon coast's ever-present fog creates dramatic, melancholy ocean views. And guests at this hostel typically come to envelop themselves in these surroundings. Hiking trails are found throughout the nearby parks, running along the cliffs and down to vast beaches the Pacific Ocean has accessorized with tide pools filled with marine life.

The hostel is full of conveniences to make vacations a little easier. Staff is on hand to rent canoes and kayaks and recommend hiking trails for all levels of experience and expertise. The front desk doubles as an espresso bar, which makes it a popular morning gathering place. It's also the place to buy a bus ticket, sign up to use the Internet-accessible computer or borrow a VCR/DVD movie.

Many guests purchase fresh-caught fish at a local seafood market and use the small kitchen to prepare a tasty dinner. After-dinner entertainment is pretty mellow: Folks gather in the common room to watch a movie. Or build a bonfire by the water out back.

All of the bedrooms are refurbished motel rooms. Dorms, outfitted with standard bunk beds, sleep 6-8 guests. Private rooms, which have private bathrooms, sleep 2-4 guests. Two private rooms have one double bed apiece. Each of five others has one double bed and one set of bunk beds. About 60% of guests are Americans who've come for a weekend getaway. This is a hostel though, so you'll not find demanding, Hawaiian-shirted tourists here. Regardless of how far they've traveled, visitors all come for the same reason – to immerse themselves in the beauty unique to the Oregon coast.

~ fast facts ~

Dorm Rates:	$16 HI members $19 non-members	**Season:**	all year
Private Rooms:	$36–$46 for 1–2 HI members; $39–$59 for 1–2 non-members	**Office Hours:**	8am–11pm
		Lock-out:	n/a
		Size:	56 beds

Credit Cards: MasterCard, Visa & Discover

Network: HI

Beds: thick foam mattresses

Kitchen: yes

Bathrooms: house-style

Lockers: yes

Extras: Internet access, onsite espresso bar, nightly movies, canoe and sea kayak rental, linen/towel rental, 1 handicapped-accessible room, laundry

Be Aware: Hostel is a refurbished motel in a working-class neighborhood. Exterior is nothing fancy, TV is used only for nightly movies.

In The Area: beaches, hikes, shopping at Cannon Beach, Astoria Column and Lewis and Clark historical sites, Seaside boardwalk

Local Tip: Buses from Seattle and Portland stop at the hostel.

Closest Free Internet: public library

Parking: free parking at hostel; bus stop nearby

is this hostel great for you?

SOLO WOMEN Yes. Small-town atmosphere. Friendly and protective staff.

PARTY ANIMALS No. A beer by the campfire is a party here. ☺

OVER 30 Yes. Amateur photographers will be in heaven on the Cannon Beach hike.

OVER 50 Yes. Couples of all ages visit from Portland and Seattle.

COUPLES Yes. Several private rooms, each with private bath.

FAMILIES Yes. Kids will like the beach and boardwalk.

GROUPS Yes, if not too large (e.g., Girl Scout troop). Group rates are available.

Troutdale, Oregon

McMENAMINS EDGEFIELD
2126 SW Halsey St.
Troutdale, OR 97060
Phone: (503) 669-8610
Fax: (503) 492-7750
E-mail: edge@mcmenamins.com
Website: www.mcmenamins.com

~ what to expect ~

Edgefield is a miniature vacation resort located just 20 minutes from downtown Portland.

The complex includes a winery (with tasting room), a movie theater, a par-3 golf course, a pub and three restaurants. Weekly concerts are given during the summer. These are hardly typical hostel offerings. But accented with shiny wood trim and soaring wall murals that decorate every hallway and stairwell, this 1911 facility is far from typical.

As you can imagine, most of the people here aren't hostelling. Roaming the grounds, in fact, you're likely to encounter more wedding guests than backpackers. Those guests will be paying nightly rates of $50–200 to occupy one of the 100 private rooms. Happily, the thoughtful owners built one women's dorm and one men's dorm to accommodate those on tighter budgets. The dorm rooms are in the same building as the other rooms, so there isn't any sense of being a second-class citizen. And guests in private rooms and dorms share the same lovely hall bathrooms.

There is one downside, though. The large dorms are well-appointed, with nightstands and rocking chairs, but sleep up to 12 people (in six sets of bunk beds). Eleven roommates is more than most people prefer. However, if you don't mind crowded rooms – or the room isn't very full – this is a really good deal. During my weekday visits, I was the only person in my dorm.

One final note: One of the owners is a huge Deadhead. An organic sculpture of Jerry Garcia has quietly graced the grounds for years, and a Jerry Garcia tribute bar recently opened. Completely unlike the rest of the complex, it's tucked away in one corner — just waiting to be found by those hiding from the mini-golf crowd. It's a dark, intimate space with a bar up front and a sitting area in back. Nothing but Grateful Dead posters on the walls and Grateful Dead concert videos on the television. Very, very cool.

~ fast facts ~

Dorm Rates: $20

Private Rooms: $50–200 (resort rooms – no private hostel rooms)

Credit Cards: MasterCard, Visa, AMEX & Discover

Network: n/a

Beds: spring mattresses

Kitchen: no

Bathrooms: shared, house-style

Lockers: no

Extras: winery, pub, restaurants, golf course, movie theater, massage, meeting facilities

Be Aware: no reservations taken for hostel beds

In The Area: Portland, Columbia River Gorge, waterfalls

Local Tip: Check out the Jerry Garcia tribute bar.

Closest Free Internet: unknown

Parking: free parking at hostel

Season: all year

Office Hours: 24 hours

Lock-out: n/a

Size: 24 bunk beds

is this hostel great for you?

SOLO WOMEN Yes. But probably more fun with a friend.

PARTY ANIMALS Yes. A winery, pub, bar and beer garden are onsite.

OVER 30 Yes. A stay in this little resort could be a welcome change, but call ahead to ensure the dorm isn't full.

OVER 50 Yes. A fun place to bring the grandkids.

COUPLES Maybe. Lots of silly, romantic activities but no private rooms at hostel rates.

FAMILIES Yes, but only in the very expensive private rooms.

GROUPS Yes, if you can fit in dorms. Lots of opportunities for fun at this little resort.

"Stop worrying about the potholes
in the road and enjoy the journey."
– *Babs Hoffman*

Pennsylvania Hostels

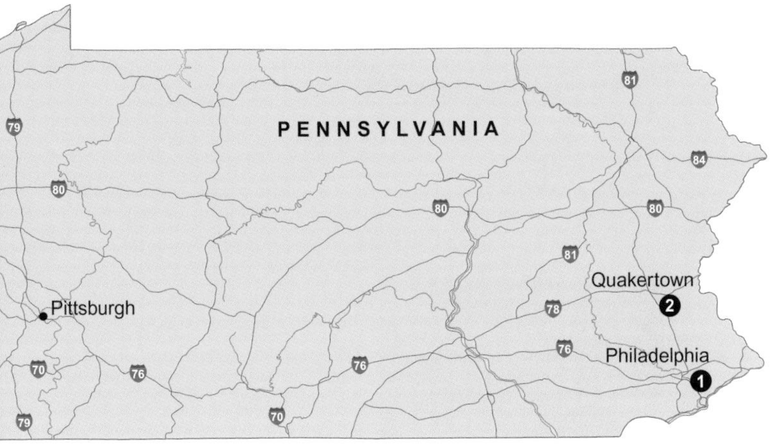

1 Philadelphia
HI – Bank Street Hostel

2 Quakertown
HI – Weisel

Philadelphia, Pennsylvania

HI – BANK STREET HOSTEL

32 S. Bank St.
Philadelphia, PA 19106
Phone: (215) 922-0222
Fax: (215) 922-4082
E-mail: manager@bankstreethostel.com
Website: www.hihostels.com

~ what to expect ~

This is a different kind of hostel. It's funky and festive, but it's not for everyone. You really need to be young and hip to fully appreciate it.

The hostel has two levels. Upstairs, you'll find the front desk, a pool table and a sitting area. Downstairs, you'll find a kitchen with yellow walls and black cabinets as well as an industrial-silver common area. Imagine a nightclub-turned-hostel.

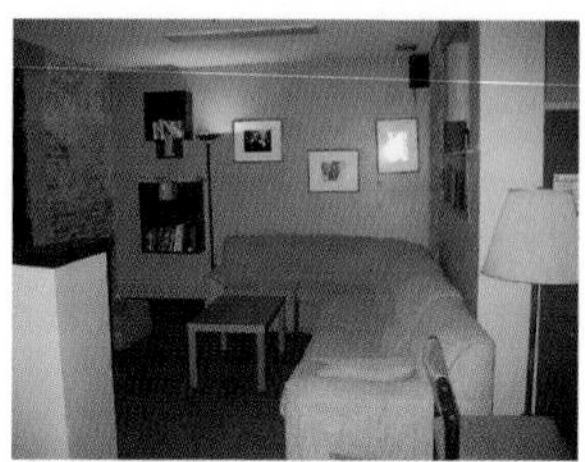

Everyone sleeps in dorm rooms here. These rooms accommodate up to 30 people and they're as clean as 30-person rooms can be. Each of the shared bathrooms has four showers, three sinks and three toilets.

The hostel is located right downtown. The location can be a little questionable at night, but it's optimal for daytime sightseeing. All the key tourist sights are nearby: the Liberty Bell, Independence Hall, the Betsy Ross House, United States Mint, Benjamin Franklin's home and workshop and more. A walk around the neighborhood is a quick lesson in American history.

~ fast facts ~

Dorm Rates: \$18 HI members
\$21 non-members

Private Rooms: n/a

Credit Cards: no

Network: HI

Beds: mix of foam & spring mattresses

Kitchen: good size, in basement

Bathrooms: shared, dorm-style

Lockers: yes, but not many

Extras: Internet access, wireless Internet, free videos, free coffee and tea, linen rental

Season: all year

Office Hours: 8am–10am & 4:30pm–12:30am

Lock-out: 10am–4:30pm

Size: 70 beds

Be Aware: The neighborhood isn't the best at night.

In The Area: Philadelphia historic sites (Liberty Bell, Independence Hall, Betsy Ross House, etc.)

Local Tip: Philadelphia has an outstanding art museum.

Closest Free Internet: public library

Parking: No free parking

is this hostel great for you?

SOLO WOMEN Yes. Don't walk alone at night, though.

PARTY ANIMALS Yes. Clubs are nearby.

OVER 30 Maybe. A bit left of center.

OVER 50 No. 30-person dorms are a bit much.

COUPLES No. No private rooms.

FAMILIES No. Not a family vibe.

GROUPS Maybe. Big enough, but certainly atypical.

Quakertown, Pennsylvania

HI – WEISEL
7347 Richlandtown Rd.
Quakertown, PA
Phone: (215) 536-8749
Fax: n/a
E-mail: n/a
Website: www.hihostels.com

~ what to expect ~

Nestled in Nockamixon State Park, the Weisel hostel is one of several HI facilities located in similar settings. As is often the case with state parks, this is a great place for city dwellers – and city travelers – to escape urban angst for a few days. The hostel is only about 90 minutes north of Philadelphia, but there's absolutely no city vibe here.

The two-story stone house is set amongst tall trees and abundant ferns and greenery drape the entranceway. Walk through the archway and enter a living space of wood beam ceilings and exposed stone walls. Sofas and chairs are grouped in front of the fireplace and a dining table and piano flank either wall. Soft touches such as antique light fixtures, Victorian-era pictures and lace doilies balance the heavy furniture and architecture. The first floor also houses a kitchen and a half-bath. Bedrooms and more bathrooms are located upstairs. Beds with thin mattresses could be more comfortable, but the rooms are clean.

The hostel is closed during the day, but a wealth of nearby attractions keeps guests busy. Visitors in need of some exercise and fresh air can hike and bike the park trails or visit the community swimming pool. Those wanting an easier day can drive to the artsy little town of New Hope for antiquing or gallery browsing. This is an ideal spot for a mellow weekend getaway.

~ fast facts ~

Dorm Rates:	$12 HI members $15 non-members
Private Rooms:	$15 per person
Credit Cards:	no
Network:	HI
Beds:	foam mattresses
Kitchen:	yes
Bathrooms:	shared, house-style
Lockers:	no
Extras:	piano, fireplace, linen rental, free Internet, group rates available
Be Aware:	plastic-covered mattresses, maximum 3-night stay
In The Area:	Nockamixon State Park hiking, biking, boating & fishing; New Hope art galleries & antique shops
Local Tip:	swimming pool at park
Closest Free Internet:	onsite
Parking:	free onsite parking
Season:	all year except Christmas week
Office Hours:	7:30am–9:30am & 4pm–10pm
Lock-out:	9:30am–4pm
Size:	20 beds

is this hostel great for you?

SOLO WOMEN Yes, but expect it to be quiet.

PARTY ANIMALS No. Park setting and alcohol ban aren't conducive to partying.

OVER 30 Yes. Check out the hip town of New Hope.

OVER 50 Yes. Mellow lodge-like atmosphere.

COUPLES Yes. Romantic setting.

FAMILIES Yes. Kids can splash in the local swimming pool.

GROUPS Yes, but only if renting the entire facility.

"The rewards of the journey far outweigh the risk of leaving the harbor."

– Unknown

Tennessee Hostels

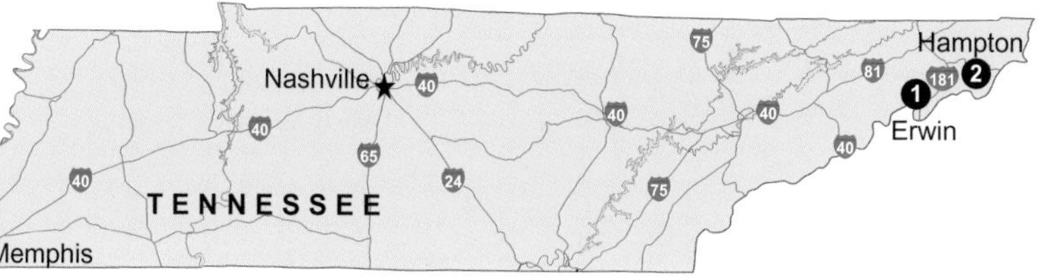

❶ **Erwin**
Uncle Johnny's Nolichucky Hostel

❷ **Hampton**
Laurel Fork Lodge

Erwin, Tennessee

UNCLE JOHNNY'S NOLICHUCKY HOSTEL
151 River Rd.
Erwin, TN 37650
Phone: (423) 735-0548
Fax: n/a
Website: www.unclejohnnys.net
E-mail: unclejohnnys2000@yahoo.com

~ what to expect ~

A hiker hostel is unlike any other. And those along the Appalachian Trail are unique even among hiker hostels.

Most hostels are permeated by an atmosphere of camaraderie created when travelers from all over the world swap stories about their adventures. At hiker hostels, you hear about adventures of a completely different nature.

Uncle Johnny's is located right on the Appalachian Trial, whose roughly 2,174-mile length runs through 14 states. As many as 4 million people hike some part of the AT each year, but only about 15% walk from one end to the other. By the time hikers reach Uncle Johnny's, they've acquired trail names, blisters and a bunch of cool stories. Those of us who can't imagine tackling a 4–7-month hike will find these folks interesting and inspiring.

Most guests are here either to hike or boat on the river, and everyone is pretty exhausted at the end of the day. So evening activities tend to consist of swinging in the hammock, eating dinner and turning in early. You find that the front porch acts as the de facto common area.

The nine-person coed dorm room is reserved for hikers. Other guests stay in private rooms in one of the cabins. Electric heaters in the cabins and a wood-burning stove in the dorm provide welcome warmth when a serious chill takes hold after sundown. A few small private rooms are furnished with bunks that have a double bed on the bottom and a single bed on top. Each of the other two is furnished with one double bed. With double bunk beds, a couch, TV, microwave and small refrigerator, the largest room is the most deluxe. Men's and women's bathrooms, which are in a separate building, have multiple sinks and toilets and two shower stalls. Additionally, there are two heated half-baths.

If you're up for a taste of what AT hikers tackle, Uncle Johnny will drive you to one of the trailheads and you can spend the day hiking back to the hostel. You may not come back with blisters or a trail name, but you can at least spin your own tale of "hiking the AT."

~ fast facts ~

Dorm Rates: $12

Private Rooms: $15–30

Credit Cards: MasterCard, Visa & AMEX

Network: n/a

Beds: foam mattresses in dorms; mix of new spring mattresses & foam mattresses in private rooms

Season: year-round

Office Hours: 7am–10pm

Lock-out: n/a

Size: 21 beds

Kitchen: limited (4 grills, 3 microwaves & 2 refrigerators); new enclosed outdoor cooking area

Bathrooms: shared, dorm-style

Lockers: no

Extras: trail shuttle service, outfitter store, sit-on-top kayak rentals, canoe rentals, tube rentals, fishing equipment, loaner bicycles and Internet access

Be Aware: Hostel dorm is coed.

In The Area: Appalachian Trail, river canoeing, kayaking, rafting & tubing, swimming beach, fishing and mountain biking

Local Tip: only 55 miles North of Asheville, NC; River's Edge restaurant with river view & frequent live music; AYCE lunch buffet; Elms Restaurant for breakfast

Closest Free Internet: Erwin public library

Parking: free onsite parking, shuttle to town & trail heads

is this hostel great for you?

SOLO WOMEN Yes. Splurge on a private room.

PARTY ANIMALS No. Mellow, outdoorsy atmosphere

OVER 30 Yes. Uncle Johnny will shuttle you up the Trail for a day hike back to the hostel.

OVER 50 Yes. The AT hikers' stories will inspire and entertain.

COUPLES Yes. Private rooms with double bed available.

FAMILIES Yes. Cabin with two private rooms can sleep up to seven people.

GROUPS Yes, if small.

Hampton, Tennessee

LAUREL FORK LODGE, LLC
1511 Dennis Cove Rd.
Hampton, TN 37658
Phone: (423) 725-5988
Fax: n/a
E-mail: lclodge@usit.net
Website: www.laurelcreeklodge.com

~ what to expect ~

Located just off the Appalachian Trail, this hostel is unique for the area. Most trail hostels are small, intimate, fairly unrefined facilities. Laurel Fork Lodge, on the other hand, is large and home to a fairly sophisticated complex of buildings.

There are two distinct sections of the property – the "hiker hostel" and the rest. The hiker hostel houses a coed dorm room and a small common kitchen. Catering to people accustomed to camping outdoors, these rooms are predictably basic.

"The rest" includes several private cabins, two lodges, a conference center and an amphitheater. This property has clearly been designed to accommodate large groups for meetings, conferences and family reunions. A hot tub, store, laundry and shuttle service are available to all guests, and the facilities are top-notch.

Hiking is the major attraction here. However, you can also catch the shuttle to nearby Watauga Lake to swim, fish or rent a pontoon boat. Or take your own car on an hour-long drive to Asheville, North Carolina, home of traditional bluegrass/roots music and the Biltmore Estate.

This is one of very few hostels in the book in which I wasn't able to spend a night: I happened upon the facility at a time when my schedule just wouldn't allow an overnight stay. But after exploring the grounds, cabins, conference center and other buildings, I couldn't, in good conscience, exclude it from a list of the best hostels in the United States.

~ fast facts ~

Dorm Rates: $6/bed in bunkhouse, $12/bed in cabin

Season: all year

Office Hours: varies

Lock-out: n/a

Size: 60 beds

Private Rooms: $25–100 cabins; rooms in lodge: $55 for 1 or 2, $65 for 3, $75 for 4; rent entire lodge for $250–350 (sleeps 16)

Credit Cards: MasterCard & Visa

Network: n/a

Beds: spring mattresses

Kitchen: yes, one for hikers and another in conference center

Bathrooms: bathhouse for bunks and cabins, shared house-style bath in lodge

Lockers: no

Extras: conference center ($100 fee – holds 100), amphitheater, laundry, campsites, RV hook-ups, pay phone, free Internet access, linen rentals, tent & RV site

Be Aware: Individuals could feel lost when a group moves in.

In The Area: Appalachian Trail hiking, lake boating, fishing, Asheville, NC & Biltmore Estate 1 hour away

Local Tip: Laurel Fork will hold mail for AT hikers.

Closest Free Internet: onsite

Parking: free onsite parking; shuttle service

is this hostel great for you?

SOLO WOMEN Yes. Check out the hot tub.

PARTY ANIMALS No. A place of outdoor adventures, not wild parties.

OVER 30 Yes. Rent a pontoon boat on Watauga Lake.

OVER 50 Yes. Hiker hostel, cabins and conference center attract a varied clientele.

COUPLES Yes. Cabins available.

FAMILIES Yes. Two available lodges sleep six and 10 people.

GROUPS Yes. The lodges and conference center are ideal for groups.

"We wander for distraction, but
we travel for fulfillment."

– *Hilaire Belloc*

Texas Hostels

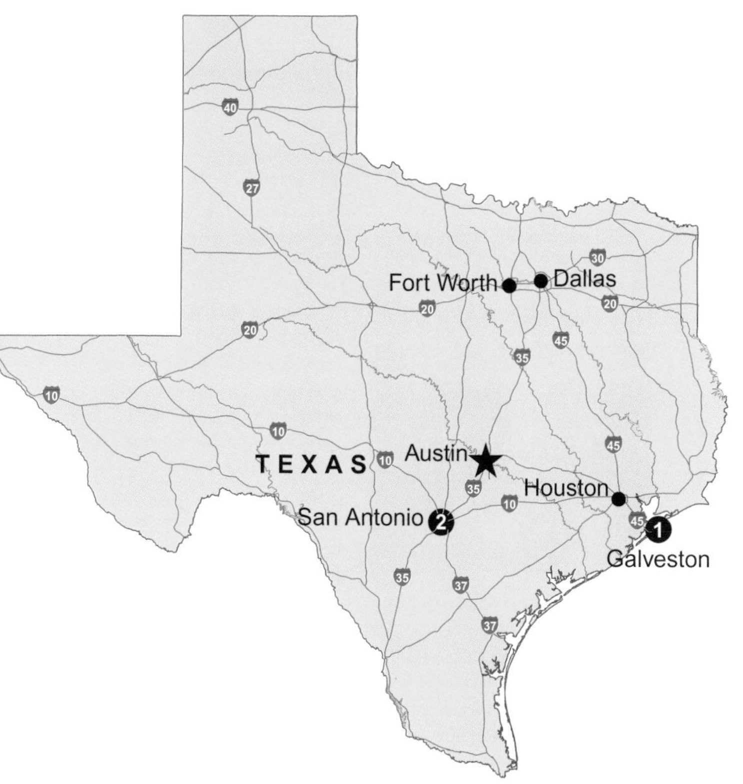

❶ **Galveston**
HI – Galveston
(Sandpiper Motel & Hostel)

❷ **San Antonio**
San Antonio International Hostel

Galveston, Texas

HI – GALVESTON
(SANDPIPER MOTEL & HOSTEL)
201 Seawall
Galveston, TX
Phone: (409) 765-9431
Fax: (409) 765-6545
E-mail: sandpiper325@aol.com
Website: www.sandpipermotel.com

~ what to expect ~

This pleasant little beachside motel has converted two of its larger rooms into hostel dorms. Unlike some other motel-hostel combinations, though, the hostel isn't treated as an afterthought. Management here actually cares about hostellers' experiences during their stay.

The hostel dorms and common areas are all in the main building, and their location contributes to the communal hostel atmosphere. Separate buildings house the motel rooms.

Each gender-segregated hostel dorm sleeps five guests in bunk beds and one double bed. The carpets are worn and the rooms are simple, but each has a balcony, a color TV and a small refrigerator.

The common areas include a small but adequate kitchen that opens into a spacious living room that's rich in windows. Guests may enjoy their meals at the kitchen bar or at one of the tables in the dining area. Nothing is fancy here, but it's a clean and comfortable place to hang out.

Most Sandpiper guests spend their days at the beach or by the pool. If you aren't a sun worshipper, you can head for The Strand. A free trolley runs between the beach and that downtown historic district.

~ fast facts ~

Dorm Rates: $18.50 HI members
$21.50 non-members

Private Rooms: none in hostel
($45–120 motel rooms)

Credit Cards: MasterCard, Visa, Discover

Network: HI

Beds: spring mattresses

Kitchen: small, but adequate

Bathrooms: private, house-style

Lockers: no

Season: all year

Office Hours: 24 hours

Lock-out: n/a

Size: 24 beds, plus traditional motel rooms

Extras: pool, TV, free laundry, piano, meeting room for 50

Be Aware: HI membership may be required in summer – call ahead.

In The Area: beach, Texas Seaport Museum, railroad museum, Texas Aviation Hall of Fame, Offshore Drilling Rig and Museum, Moody Gardens, deep sea fishing, boat cruise in harbor, sea turtle-rearing facility

Local Tip: Galveston hosts the largest Marti Gras festival in Texas (February); 30,000 lbs. of ice is used to create snow for the Christmas Festival in December.

Closest Free Internet: public library – 25th & Broadway

Parking: free, onsite parking; bus between beach & business district

is this hostel great for you?

SOLO WOMEN Yes. However, you may be the only hosteller in low season.

PARTY ANIMALS Yes. Good road-trip destination.

OVER 30 Yes. Good beach location and onsite pool make for a nice getaway.

OVER 50 Yes. Several shops, attractions and museums are located in Galveston.

COUPLES No. No hostel private rooms available.

FAMILIES No. No hostel family rooms.

GROUPS No. Hostel rooms sleep only a total of 10.

San Antonio, Texas

SAN ANTONIO INTERNATIONAL HOSTEL

P.O. Box 8059
621 Pierce St.
San Antonio, TX 78208
Phone: (210) 223-9426
Fax: (210) 299-1479
E-mail: hisananton@aol.com
Website: n/a

~ what to expect ~

One of the best cities in Texas, San Antonio celebrates traditional and contemporary Hispanic culture. Remembering to visit the Alamo is mandatory for anyone interested in history, but don't forget to check out a few of the other, lesser-known missions on the edge of town. Each is unique and memorable.

After that brief history lesson, head back downtown to the River Walk. Cobblestone paths, shops and restaurants line the banks here, where the San Antonio River threads its way through the heart of the city. Boats ply the water while pedestrians stroll along the paths of this famous tourist attraction. Be sure to sample the margaritas, enchiladas and salsa at any of the several good Mexican restaurants in this area.

The hostel is located in a residential neighborhood 10 minutes from downtown. A 1970s décor prevails throughout the hostel, which features a small common room and kitchen. Simple dorms and private rooms share bathrooms.

The owners also operate The Bullis House. Located next door to the hostel, this B&B is a meticulously restored historic home whose rooms are decorated with lace curtains and antique furniture. On slow days, management has been known to offer a hostel discount on the rate of the smallest room. Feel free to inquire – but exercise good sense and arrive looking presentable.

It's kind of a shame hostellers must check in at The Bullis House. The hostel is OK, but it seems awfully bare in comparison to its fancy neighbor. Perhaps as consolation, guests of both facilities may use the backyard swimming pool. It, and the air conditioning, can be godsends during sweltering Texas summers.

~ fast facts ~

Dorm Rates: $23

Private Rooms: $39–$46 (1 or 2 people)

Credit Cards: MasterCard & Visa

Network: n/a

Beds: spring mattresses

Kitchen: yes

Bathrooms: shared, dorm-style

Lockers: yes

Extras: swimming pool, breakfast available, air conditioning, linen rental

Season: year-round

Office Hours: 8am–10pm

Lock-out: n/a

Size: 38 beds

Be Aware: not within walking distance of attractions

In The Area: the Alamo, Spanish missions, River Walk shopping & dining area

Local Tip: Small B&B room may be discounted for HI members during slow seasons.

Closest Free Internet: public library – 1½ miles away

Parking: free onsite parking

is this hostel great for you?

SOLO WOMEN Yes. If you have a car.

PARTY ANIMALS No. Not at all.

OVER 30 Yes. Bring your swimsuit to enjoy the pool.

OVER 50 No. Check next door.

COUPLES Yes. But inquire next door.

FAMILIES No. An inexpensive motel would be a better value.

GROUPS No. Not especially well-suited for groups.

"If you wish to travel far and fast, travel light. Take off all your envies, jealousies, unforgiveness, selfishness, and fears."

– *Glenn Clark*

Utah Hostels

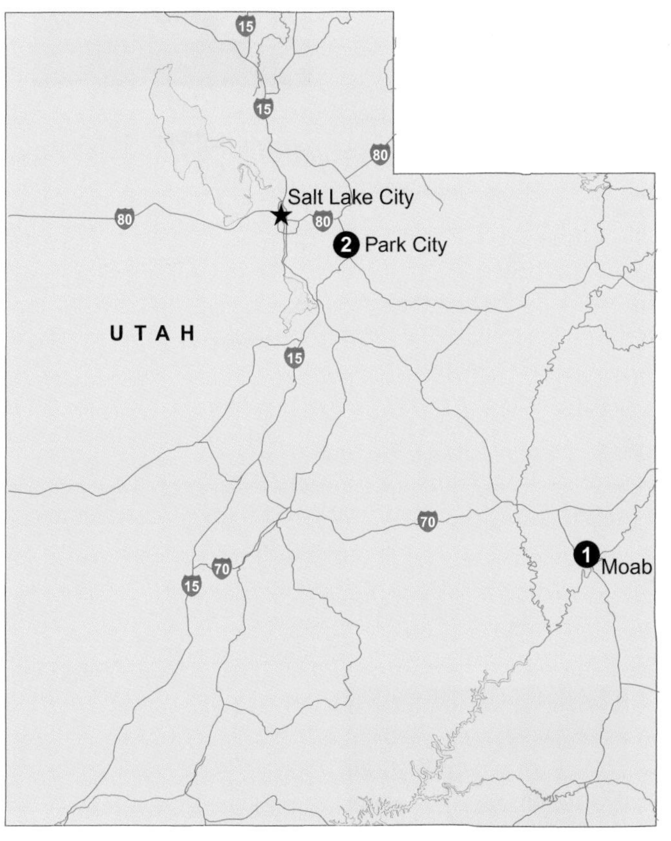

1 Moab
Center Street Hotel & Hostel

2 Park City
Base Camp

Moab, Utah

CENTER STREET HOTEL & HOSTEL
96 E. Center St.
Moab, UT 84532
Phone: (888) 530-3134 or
(435) 259-9431
Fax: (435) 250-8488
E-mail: kokopeli@lasal.net
Website: www.kokopellilodge.com

~ what to expect ~

This hostel doesn't yet have all its ducks in a row. But it's the best hostel available in an outstanding location.

Lovers of extreme sports flock to Moab. It's the Holy Grail for climbers and mountain bikers who come to test their skill on the slick rock. Hikers join them in exploring Utah's red rock formations in two nearby national parks, Canyonlands and The Arches.

Other than the location, the best aspect of this hostel is its fun bedrooms. The spacious, clean, comfortable private rooms feature theme décors – safari, 1950s, etc. A blue mural depicting life in the sea covers the walls of the only dorm. Rooms are air-conditioned and guests sleep on firm spring mattresses in twin beds, rather than in bunks.

All guests share hall bathrooms outfitted with two sinks, toilets and showers. While cleaned regularly, they'd benefit from fresh paint, new shower curtains and the like.

The common areas also need some work. The front room that serves as the main common room is furnished with a table and few older chairs. The small attached kitchen is fairly old and not stocked with dishes or pots and pans. The biggest problem the owners need to address, however, is the unpleasant odor that lingers in the hallway and throughout the common area. Not surprisingly, the smell puts a damper on socializing. It was absent in the bedrooms, but it needs to be eliminated throughout the hostel.

This isn't yet a great hostel, but it's a great location. And with any luck, the new owners will soon get a handle on the things that require their attention. In the meantime, this is still the hostel of choice in Moab.

~ fast facts ~

Dorm Rates:	$15	**Season:**	all year
Private Rooms:	$40 for 2, $5 for each additional person	**Office Hours:**	8am–9pm
		Lock-out:	n/a
Credit Cards:	MasterCard, Visa, Discover & AMEX	**Size:**	21 beds
Network:	n/a		
Beds:	spring mattresses		
Kitchen:	yes		
Bathrooms:	shared, dorm-style		
Lockers:	no		
Extras:	free linens & towels, free coffee		

Be Aware: Check-in is at the Kokopelli Lodge (100 East).

In The Area: mountain biking, climbing, hiking, rafting, Canyonlands and Arches National Parks

Local Tip: Mondo Café for great, strong coffee; Red Rocks for breakfast & bakery; Eddie McStiffs for food & beer

Closest Free Internet: public library across the street

Parking: free street parking

is this hostel great for you?

This hostel's location and bedrooms are stellar. Other elements need to be corrected, though.

Park City, Utah

BASE CAMP
268 Main St.
Park City Utah 84060
Phone: (888) 980-7244
Fax: n/a
E-mail: info@parkcitybasecamp.com
Website: www.parkcitybasecamp.com

~ what to expect ~

Located less than 45 minutes from Salt Lake City, Park City is an upscale resort town that caters primarily to the ski crowd. The town, and the hostel, bustle with activity during the winter when skiers, snowboarders and snowshoers arrive to revel in some of the best snow in America.

Unlike most hostels in ritzy destinations, though, this one isn't located on some back street in a dodgy part of town. In fact, it couldn't be in a better spot: right on Main Street in the midst of the town's best coffee shops, shopping boutiques, restaurants and pubs. (Conservative Mormon influences have less impact in Park City than they do in Salt Lake City.)

This isn't a hostel where guests hang around and get to know each other during the day. The common room is small, seriously lacking in furniture and not very conducive to socializing. It's an oversight I can overlook, though, because visitors don't generally come to Park City to sit inside.

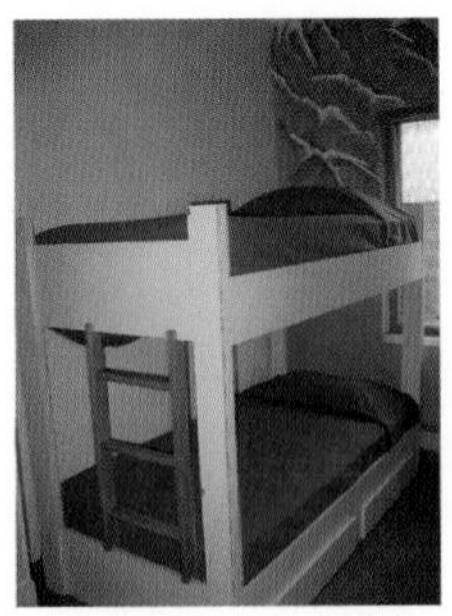

Each bedroom is furnished with a desk and two sets of white, wood bunk beds. During the ski season, most of the 70 beds are filled with guys under the age of 30.

Common areas are minimal, but walls brightened with landscape murals keep the hostel feeling fresh and new. A small kitchen is available for those who can't afford to treat themselves to the wonderful restaurants nearby – or who would rather spend their money on the slopes or in the bar.

If you prefer a more serene experience, visit Park City during the summer. I had a room all to myself in August. The town is actively trying to promote hiking, biking, fly fishing, horseback riding, white water rafting and other warm-weather pastimes, but the effort hasn't yet taken hold. Access to a car is important in the off-season, when the shuttles don't run between town and the ski resorts.

Regardless of when you visit, there is plenty of good eating, drinking and outdoor fun to be had in Park City. And, just as the name promises, Base Camp is a good temporary abode from which to explore it all.

~ fast facts ~

Dorm Rates: $25 in summer
$35 in winter

Private Rooms: $85 in summer
$105 in winter

Credit Cards: MasterCard, Visa, Discover & AMEX

Network: n/a

Beds: bunks with spring mattresses

Kitchen: yes

Bathrooms: dorm style

Lockers: no

Season: all year

Office Hours: 2pm–9pm

Lock-out: n/a

Size: 62 beds

Extras: free linens & towels; free Internet; color TV, VCR, laundry, ADA room

Be Aware: no air conditioning, limited common room

In The Area: skiing, snowboarding, hiking, biking, fishing, wakeboarding, jet ski rental, shopping

Local Tip: Local paper has discount coupons for high-end restaurants; cheap film series at the library.

Closest Free Internet: onsite

Parking: paid garage parking near hostel;
$40 RT shuttle from airport

is this hostel great for you?

SOLO WOMEN Yes. Upscale town, safe location.

PARTY ANIMALS Yes. Bars within stumble-home distance. More action in the winter.

OVER 30 Yes. Great place to meet sophisticated locals and visitors.

OVER 50 Yes. Summer quieter than winter.

COUPLES Maybe. Location has romantic possibilities, but hostel private rooms have bunk beds.

FAMILIES Maybe. Families of four or fewer might enjoy the summer season.

GROUPS Not especially. Small kitchen/dining area.

"The most important trip you may take in life is meeting people halfway."

– *Henry Boye*

Vermont Hostels

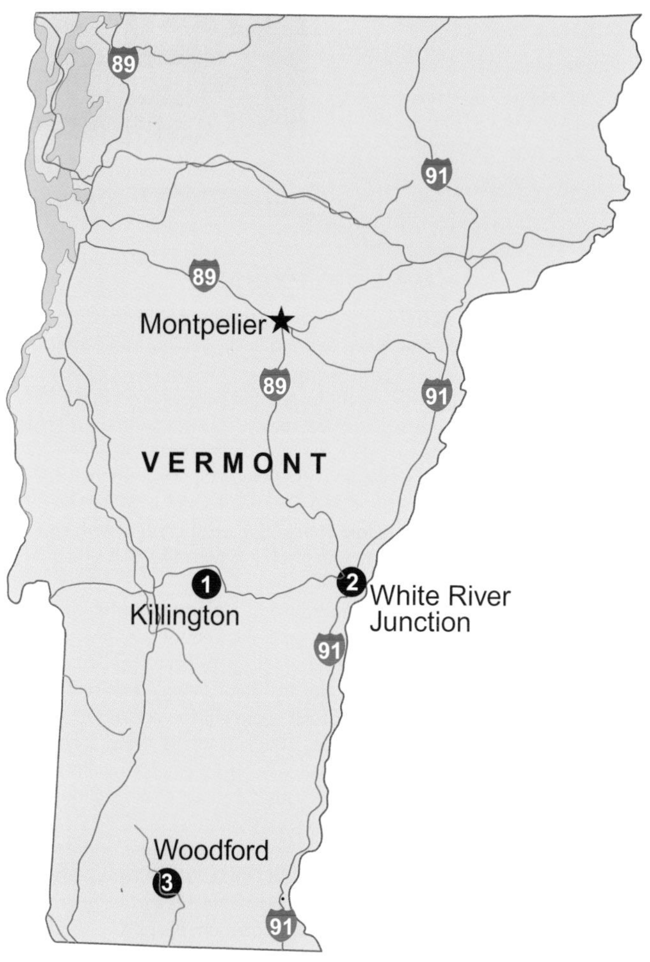

❶ **Killington**
Turn of River Lodge

❷ **White River Junction**
HI – White River Junction (Hotel Coolidge)

❸ **Woodford**
HI – Greenwood Lodge Hostel & Camping

Killington, Vermont

TURN OF RIVER LODGE
5672 U.S. Route. 4
P.O. Box 257
Killington, VT 05751
Phone: (802) 422-3766 or
(800) 782-9867
Fax: (802) 422-3767
E-mail: n/a
Website: wwww.turnofriverlodge.com

~ what to expect ~

Killington is one of the most popular vacation destinations on the East Coast, especially during the autumn "leaf-peeping" and winter ski seasons.

Vermont is known for the beautiful red and yellow leaves that adorn its trees in the fall. At the height of the season, cars packed with amateur photographers line the local two-lane roads. Hostellers who visit Killington at this time of year will find the crowd a bit older and comprised largely of couples looking for a little weekend romance. Winter, on the other hand, attracts a decidedly younger, more spirited crowd whose members come to ski at the popular resort just two miles down the road from the hostel.

Regardless of the season, Turn of River is a wonderful place to stay when you visit Vermont. A large stone fireplace and cushy overstuffed furniture fill the first-floor living room and New England charm fills every room of the lodge. Attached to the living room are a small ski work room and a dining area where guests enjoy a free continental breakfast.

Sleeping accommodations include several dorm rooms with sturdy wood bunk beds, side tables and reading lamps. Private rooms are also available. All beds have comfortable spring mattresses and are pre-made with quilts or fuzzy blankets. One family dorm room sleeps seven and has a private attached bath. A cabin next to the main building sleeps 11.

Those planning a trip to Killington during the summer or spring months shouldn't worry about missing the high season. The quieter months can be an even richer experience. Because there are fewer guests at the hostel, everyone receives more personal attention. You may even get upgraded to a nicer room! Spring is an especially smart time to visit. As locals are quick to point out, the subtle differences in the new leaves' shades of green are every bit as beautiful as the autumn colors.

~ fast facts ~

Dorm Rates: $15–36

Private Rooms: $25–160 (1 or 2 people)

Credit Cards: MasterCard, Visa, AMEX & Discover

Network: n/a

Beds: spring mattresses

Kitchen: microwave only

Bathrooms: private and shared

Lockers: no

Extras: fireplace, TV, game room, ski work room, free continental breakfast, reduced group rates

Season: all year

Office Hours: 3pm–11pm

Lock-out: n/a

Size: 90 beds

Be Aware: Dorm space may be coed; strict cancellation policy.

In The Area: 2 miles from Killington ski resort

Local Tip: free buses to ski resorts

Closest Free Internet: Killington public library

Parking: free onsite parking

is this hostel great for you?

SOLO WOMEN Yes. Management is fun and friendly.

PARTY ANIMALS Yes, in winter. Really quiet in slower seasons.

OVER 30 Yes. Great New England ski lodge atmosphere.

OVER 50 Yes. Check out the trees in fall and spring.

COUPLES Yes. Cozy private rooms available.

FAMILIES Yes. Ski season would be too rowdy in the dorms, though.

GROUPS Yes. Separate cabin sleeps 11.

White River Junction, Vermont

HI – WHITE RIVER JUNCTION (HOTEL COOLIDGE)
39 S. Main St.
P.O. Box 515
White River Junction, VT 05001
Phone: (802) 295-3118 or
(800) 622-1124
Fax: (802) 291-5100
E-mail: info@hotelcollidge.com
Website: www.hotelcoolidge.com

~ what to expect ~

The Hotel Coolidge is just as lovely and comfortable as you'd expect a family-run Vermont inn to be. It also has a long and interesting history, having offered guest accommodations since 1849.

In its present incarnation, the hotel primarily focuses on events (weddings, banquets, conferences, etc.) and the 96 private guest-rooms. However, the service the staff provides certainly doesn't reflect what a very small part of its business the hostel represents. Hostellers are treated with respect and welcomed as warmly as guests staying in the higher-price rooms.

The hostel common area isn't much to speak of – a small kitchen with a TV in the corner. But there isn't much reason to spend time there, anyway. The nice onsite Internet café and coffeehouse is the place to log on and wind down.

Hostel rooms aren't dorms. They're private rooms that sleep one or two and provide more privacy than most. All guests share the private hall bathrooms.

This is a lovely part of the country at every time of year. Winter brings skiers. Spring and summer bring hikers and antiquers. And fall is the season of the "leaf-peepers" (people who come to see the beautiful colors of the foliage). Those less interested in nature will find quaint gift shops, cheese shops and maple syrup factories to explore.

~ fast facts ~

Dorm Rates:	$19 HI members $29 non-members
Private Rooms:	$19 for 1 HI member $29 for 1 non-member $39 for 2 HI members $49 for 2 non-members
Season:	all year
Office Hours:	24 hour
Lock-out:	n/a
Size:	26 beds
Credit Cards:	MasterCard, Visa, Discover & AMEX
Network:	HI
Beds:	spring mattresses
Kitchen:	small
Bathrooms:	shared, house-style
Lockers:	no
Extras:	onsite Internet café
Be Aware:	Hostel is a small part of the hotel's business.
In The Area:	skiing, Vermont dairies, maple syrup producers, Dartmouth University
Local Tip:	The green spring foliage is every bit as wonderful as colors in the fall.
Closest Free Internet:	onsite café
Parking:	free onsite parking; shuttle service

is this hostel great for you?

SOLO WOMEN Yes. Lovely inn atmosphere.

PARTY ANIMALS No. Too quiet.

OVER 30 Yes. Hostellers, hotel guests and locals mingle in the café.

OVER 50 Yes. A great place for history or nature buffs.

COUPLES Yes. Hostel rooms offer privacy for two.

FAMILIES No. No hostel facilities for families.

GROUPS Not in hostel. Hotel is perfect for groups, however.

Woodford, Vermont

HI – GREENWOOD LODGE HOSTEL & CAMPING

VT Highway 9, Prospect Access Rd.
P.O. Box 246
Woodford, VT 05201
Phone: (802) 442-2547 phone
Fax: (802) 442-2547
E-mail: campgreenwood@aol.com
Website: www.hihostels.com

~ what to expect ~

The hardwood floors, beam ceilings and mounted deer head inside this lodge serve as reminders that you're in a mountain locale. Canoes and rowboats are provided so guests can paddle in the two ponds that lie just beyond the main building. And hikers will enjoy forging a path through the tree-covered mountains.

The hostel sleeps 20, but tent and RV campsites provide room for many more guests. The dorm rooms share bathrooms with multiple sinks, toilets and showers. Women sleep in twin-bedded rooms; men get a mix of twin beds and bunk beds. (Unfortunately, thin foam mattresses covered in plastic may prevent you from getting a good night's sleep. Greenwood is one of several hostels that use these very hygienic but very uncomfortable covers.)

This small lodge also houses a communal kitchen, dining room and common room. The spotless, well-equipped kitchen is available for all guests to use and meals can be eaten at one of the two long tables in the dining room. While a television and piano can be found in the common room, conversation with the owners will prove more interesting and entertaining. Ed and Ann have owned the place for decades and have spent many years hosting programs for kids and conducting outings for troubled teens. Now that they've retired from their day jobs and head south for a few months each year, the hostel is no longer open during the winter ski season. That's too bad. Be sure to visit them in the spring or summer while you still can.

~ fast facts ~

Dorm Rates:	$21 HI members $23 non-members	**Season:**	mid-May– late October
Private Rooms:	$45–50	**Office Hours:**	9am–9pm
Credit Cards:	no	**Lock-out:**	n/a
Network:	HI	**Size:**	17 beds

Beds: thin foam mattresses with plastic covers in dorm, spring mattresses in private rooms

Kitchen: good size

Bathrooms: shared, dorm-style

Lockers: no

Extras: piano, free canoes and rowboats, tent/RV campsites, campfire kindling for sale, modem hook-ups

Be Aware: Frying anything greasy is not allowed; closed during winter ski season.

In The Area: hiking, biking, historical sites, covered bridges

Local Tip: 3 miles from the Appalachian Trail and Long Trail

Closest Free Internet: Bennington public library

Parking: free onsite parking

is this hostel great for you?

SOLO WOMEN Yes. Very safe mountain area.

PARTY ANIMALS No. Quiet hostel eight miles from town.

OVER 30 Yes. Guests are a mix of Americans and international students, but tend to be older than typical hostel guests.

OVER 50 Yes. The owners are a very interesting and friendly retired couple.

COUPLES Yes. Private rooms available.

FAMILIES Yes. Kids will love evening bonfires and daytime canoeing.

GROUPS Yes. Many campsites available in addition to the hostel.

"Travel is fatal to prejudice, bigotry, and narrow-mindedness, and many of our people need it sorely on these accounts. Broad, wholesome, charitable views of men and things cannot be acquired by vegetating in one little corner of the earth all one's lifetime."

– Mark Twain

Virginia Hostels

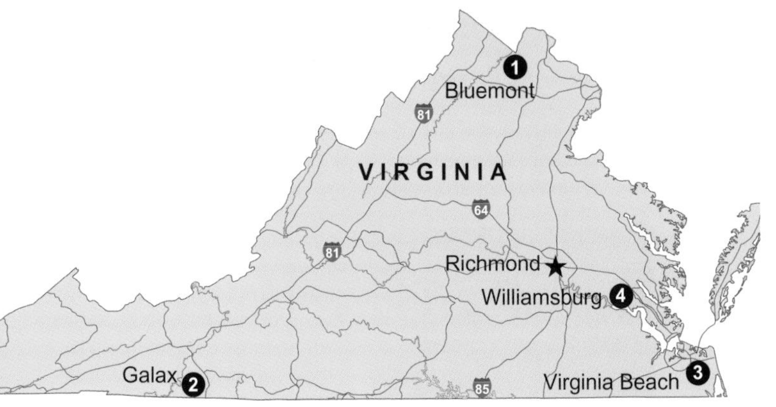

1. **Bluemont**
   Bears Den Hostel
2. **Galax**
   Hostel Blue Ridge Mountains
3. **Virginia Beach**
   HI – Angie's Guest Cottage
4. **Williamsburg**
   Mrs. Carter's Home Hostel

Bluemont, Virginia

BEARS DEN HOSTEL
18393 Blueridge Mtn. Rd.
Bluemont, VA 20135
Phone: (540) 554-8708
Fax: n/a
E-mail: info@bearsdencenter.org
Website: www.bearsdencenter.org

~ what to expect ~

Guests who arrive at Bears Den may wonder if they've stepped into a fairy tale. The big stone house, set among the pine trees and the Blue Ridge Mountains, could certainly be the setting for one.

This atmospheric hostel is a favorite with hikers passing through on the nearby Appalachian Trail or just up for a weekend outing or day hike. Backpackers taking a break from the Trail even receive a discount on their dorm accommodations.

The hostel's sturdy stone walls infuse the rooms with character, and sun-filled windows keep them from becoming too dark and heavy. The common rooms include a living room, dining room and kitchen. A stone fireplace dominates the living room, as the big wood table does the dining room. Both rooms are big enough to accommodate small groups.

Most guests stay in dorm rooms outfitted with twin bunks. However, the one available private room sleeps six, with one double bed and two sets of twin bunk beds. A small cottage on the grounds can also be rented. Either is a good option for small families or group leaders.

~ fast facts ~

Dorm Rates:	$18 ($6 children under 13)	**Season:**	March–November
Private Rooms:	$50 (1 or 2 people) $15 each add'l adult, $6 each add'l child	**Office Hours:**	5pm–10pm
		Lock-out:	9am–5pm
		Size:	26 beds
Credit Cards:	MasterCard & Visa		
Network:	n/a		
Beds:	mixed in dorms, spring mattresses in private		
Kitchen:	yes		
Bathrooms:	private, dorm-style		
Lockers:	yes		
Extras:	store with food & souvenirs, laundry, fireplace, free linens, camping, cottage, hiking, organic garden		
Be Aware:	not much to do if you don't like the outdoors		
In The Area:	Appalachian Trail hiking, river tubing		
Local Tip:	$5 discount in dorms for backpackers who come directly from the Appalachian Trail		
Closest Free Internet:	public library, 15 minutes away		
Parking:	free onsite parking		

is this hostel great for you?

SOLO WOMEN Yes. Friendly, intimate setting.

PARTY ANIMALS No. Not much for you here.

OVER 30 Yes. Especially if you're a hiker.

OVER 50 Yes. Onsite organic garden yields produce for guests.

COUPLES Maybe. Nice setting, but no "couples rooms."

FAMILIES Yes. One six-person private room is available.

GROUPS Yes. It's possible to rent the entire 26-bed facility.

Galax, Virginia

HOSTEL BLUE RIDGE MOUNTAINS
214507 Blue Ridge Pkwy.
Galax, VA 24333
Phone: (276) 236-4962
Fax: n/a
E-mail: n/a
Website: n/a

~ what to expect ~

The Blue Ridge Mountains and their smoky-blue shadows envelop this hostel and create an environment especially fitting for the home of Appalachian bluegrass music.

Appalachian music, which tells the often-difficult life stories of down-to-earth, hardworking folks who love their families and love their land, has experienced a popular resurgence in the past few years. If you are a fan – or if you're up for a new experience – check out some live music at the nearby Blue Ridge Music Center. The hostel owner keeps the Center's schedule on hand.

Located in the top floor of the owner's colonial house, the hostel affords panoramic views of the mountains. The vista from the back common room is especially striking.

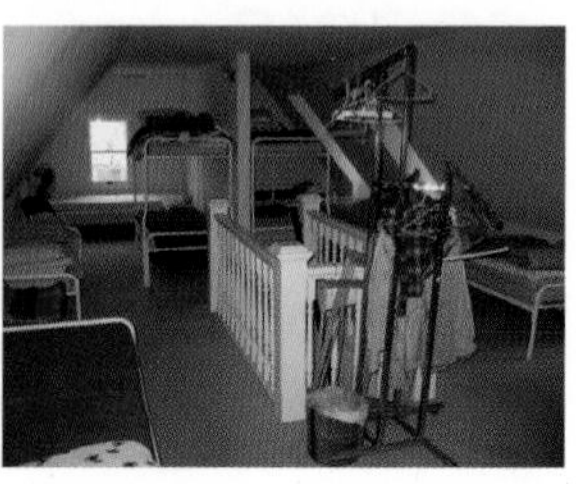

The A-frame roofline and abundant windows along the back common room create a sunny attic atmosphere throughout the common areas of this hostel. Tables and chairs are set up for dining in the common room and kitchen. Bathrooms are off the hallway, and guests sleep in men's and women's dorm rooms that are comfortable, though simple and somewhat dated.

~ fast facts ~

Dorm Rates:	$20
Private Rooms:	n/a
Credit Cards:	no
Network:	n/a
Beds:	foam mattresses
Kitchen:	yes
Bathrooms:	shared, house-style
Lockers:	no
Extras:	linens for rent
Be Aware:	not easy to reach via public transportation
In The Area:	Blue Ridge Mountain hiking and canoeing
Local Tip:	traditional Appalachian music at the Blue Ridge Music Center
Closest Free Internet:	unknown
Parking:	free onsite parking
Season:	April–October (open to groups year-round)
Office Hours:	7am–9:30am & 5–10pm
Lock-out:	9:30am–5pm
Size:	20 beds

is this hostel great for you?

SOLO WOMEN Maybe. Really safe, but really quiet.

PARTY ANIMALS No, not at all.

OVER 30 Yes. Simple but comfortable.

OVER 50 Yes. Be sure to check out the Blue Ridge Music Center.

COUPLES No. No private rooms available.

FAMILIES No. No family accommodations.

GROUPS Yes, but only if you rent the entire facility.

Virginia Beach, Virginia

HI – ANGIE'S GUEST COTTAGE
302 24th St.
Virginia Beach, VA 23451
Phone: (757) 428-4690
Fax: (757) 428-8087
E-mail: n/a
Website: www.angiescottage.com

~ what to expect ~

Angie's is one of my favorite beach hostels. People will find lots of good fun here.

Visitors come to Virginia Beach for the sun and sand – and the town knows it. Everything is kept in top condition. You can spread out a beach towel and recline on the sand or just stroll along the beachside boardwalk and enjoy the view. The town's trolley system can shuttle you to shops and attractions farther afield.

Angie's guests will find it easy to join the fun. The beach is just two blocks from the hostel and $2 day privileges are offered for the day you check out. (Day privileges allow guests to store luggage at Angie's and shower after one final afternoon of sun, sand and surf.)

Guests can continue to take advantage of the stellar weather even after returning from the beach. A landscaped backyard courtyard is outfitted with hammocks, picnic tables, reclining sun chairs and a pingpong table. The kitchen is very small, so groups will want to make use of the large charcoal grill for outdoor cooking. Aside from a couple of couches in the front lobby, Angie's doesn't really have any indoor common areas.

Everyone sleeps on a twin bunk in one of the dorms, and savvy guests choose upper bunks. (The real mattresses on these beds are far more comfortable than the thin foam ones on the lower bunks.) Be aware that the rooms have multiple fans, but no air conditioning.

~ fast facts ~

Dorm Rates:	$13.70	**Season:**	April–October
Private Rooms:	$32.60	**Office Hours:**	10am–9pm
Credit Cards:	MasterCard & Visa	**Lock-out:**	9:30am–5pm
Network:	HI	**Size:**	34 beds

Beds: spring & foam mattresses (covered in plastic)

Kitchen: small indoor kitchen, large charcoal grill outside

Bathrooms: attached, house-style

Lockers: yes

Extras: pingpong table, hammocks, sun porch, use of showers and luggage storage for $2/day

Be Aware: No air conditioning; surcharge for credit cards; guests MUST have an HI membership, international student ID card or valid passport.

In The Area: beach and boardwalk just 2 blocks away

Local Tip: good trolley system in town

Closest Free Internet: public library

Parking: free parking w/$20 deposit for permit

is this hostel great for you?

SOLO WOMEN Yes. Only blocks from the beach.

PARTY ANIMALS Yes. Party in town, though. No alcohol allowed in the hostel.

OVER 30 Yes. Town is nice, not tourist-tacky.

OVER 50 Yes. May want to splurge for B&B room, though.

COUPLES Not especially, but can stay in coed dorm.

FAMILIES No. Limited privacy.

GROUPS Yes, if small. Will need to grill outside, though, due to small kitchen size.

Williamsburg, Virginia

MRS. CARTER'S HOME HOSTEL
903 Lafayette
Williamsburg, VA 23185
Phone: (757) 229-1117
Fax: n/a
E-mail: n/a
Website: n/a

~ what to expect ~

Road-weary travelers may find a stay at Mrs. Carter's to be just what the doctor ordered.

Mrs. Carter and her husband are a quiet older couple who now use the second floor of their home as a hostel. The rest of the home is their private residence.

Upstairs, hostellers will find two spacious and homelike private rooms and one bathroom. Decorated in keeping with the rest of the house, each bedroom features wood-framed floral prints, frilly lace curtains, an antique dresser and a sitting area with chairs and reading lights. A Bible rests on each nightstand. One bedroom has two twin beds and the other has two double beds. Each is made up with a fresh set of linens prior to guests' arrival. No common areas are available.

Nearby Williamsburg, Yorktown and Jamestown are major destinations for American history buffs. Jamestown and Yorktown are a short drive from the hostel, and Colonial Williamsburg is within walking distance.

A visit to Colonial Williamsburg is a step back in time. A faithful recreation of the town as it was in the 1700s, the park includes 88 original or reconstructed buildings. You can visit the courthouse, blacksmith's shop, cabinetmaker, shoemaker, and tavern, among others. Guided by interpreters wearing 16th-century dress, daily walking tours demonstrate how the town's original residents lived and worked. They're a good way to become acquainted with the most important spots.

It's nice to have a hostel nearby to help offset the park's high-priced tickets. A one-day adult pass is $40; a child's pass is $20. Value-conscious visitors will opt to add a second consecutive day for just $3 more.

Whether you come for the peace and quiet or the proximity to the park, Mrs. Carter's has what you're looking for.

~ fast facts ~

Dorm Rates: n/a

Private Rooms: $20/person

Credit Cards: no

Network: n/a

Beds: spring mattresses

Kitchen: no

Bathrooms: house-style

Lockers: no

Extras: bedside Bible

Be Aware: Hostel may close in the near future – call ahead!

In The Area: Colonial Williamsburg Historic Area

Local Tip: A 2-day pass at Colonial Williamsburg is about the same price as a 1-day pass.

Closest Free Internet: public library

Parking: street parking

Season: year-round

Office Hours: vary; closed by 10pm

Lock-out: n/a

Size: 4 beds

is this hostel great for you?

SOLO WOMEN Yes. You won't have anyone to talk with, though.

PARTY ANIMALS No. Not your scene at all. Quiet, religious owners.

OVER 30 Yes. Can visit Colonial Williamsburg, Yorktown and Jamestown from here.

OVER 50 Yes. Ask about the free evening concerts in Colonial Williamsburg.

COUPLES Yes. Can be quite romantic.

FAMILIES No. Families can probably get cheaper rooms at a motel.

GROUPS No. Hostel sleeps only six people.

"A person needs at intervals to separate from family and companions and go to new places. One must go without familiars in order to be open to influences, to change."

– *Katharine Butler Hathaway*

Washington Hostels

1 Seattle
HI – Seattle

2 Vashon Island
HI – Vashon Island
(AYH Ranch Hostel)

Seattle, Washington

HI – SEATTLE
84 Union St.
Seattle, WA 98101
Phone: (206) 622-5443 or
(888) 622-5443
Fax: (206) 682-2179
E-mail: office@hiseattle.org
Website: www.hiseattle.org

~ what to expect ~

Great seafood, bookstores and pubs are just steps from your door at the best hostel in Seattle.

Furnished with two sets of bunk beds, a chair, mirror and lockers, the clean, basic dorm rooms at HI-Seattle aren't anything to write home about. But you won't find guests sleeping on the floor, as is sometimes the case at the other hostel nearby.

What the facility lacks in charm, it makes up for in price and location. Seattle draws travelers from all parts of the world, and most of them pay $150 or more for a hotel room. Any safe, clean, well-located alternative is worth serious consideration – and that's what thousands of visitors a year give this busy hostel.

When the sun makes one of its rare appearances in Seattle, there isn't anything better than a walk through the hustle and bustle of nearby Pike Place Market. Crowds gather to watch seafood vendors toss fish and banter with bystanders. Tourists sip cappuccino from the original Starbucks coffee shop. Local artists display their watercolors of the waterfront, and ferry boats slip away from docks and head toward nearby islands.

Visitors will want to be part of that action. And this hostel, located just a block from the Market, is a good base from which to explore. Volunteers at the concierge desk in the hostel's common area provide maps, literature and recommendations. You can glean additional information by taking one of the free walking tours, which are offered daily. I joined eight other guests, age 22–60, on one of the evening walks. It was fun and informative, and I made some new friends to go out with that evening.

~ fast facts ~

Dorm Rates: $21 HI members, $24 non-members

Private Rooms: $49–59 for 2, $10 each additional person

Credit Cards: MasterCard, Visa & AMEX

Network: HI

Beds: foam mattresses

Kitchen: yes

Bathrooms: shared, dorm-style

Lockers: yes, in bedrooms

Season: all year

Office Hours: 24 hours

Lock-out: n/a: 24-hour access with key card

Size: 161 beds

Extras: free walking tours, Internet access, wireless Internet access, concierge desk, free towels and linens and free continental breakfast

Be Aware: no air conditioning, difficult parking

In The Area: Pike Place Market, aquarium, ferry rides, Elliot Bay Bookstore, underground tour, art museums, Experience Music Project interactive music museum, Space Needle Observation Deck, zoo

Local Tip: free buses in tourist section of town, half-price show tickets sold in market shop

Closest Free Internet: public library and museum

Parking: garage parking $10–15/day

is this hostel great for you?

SOLO WOMEN Yes. Free walking tours are a good way to meet other solo travelers.

PARTY ANIMALS Yes. This city rocks! Pretty quiet hostel, though.

OVER 30 Yes. An interesting, well-traveled clientele.

OVER 50 Yes. Hostellers age 20–70 stay here regularly.

COUPLES Maybe. It's difficult to secure a private room here.

FAMILIES Maybe. Younger children will need close supervision.

GROUPS Yes. Large kitchen and dining areas are well-suited for groups.

Vashon Island, Washington

HI – VASHON ISLAND
(AYH RANCH HOSTEL)
Vashon Island, WA 98070
Phone: (206) 463-2592
Fax: (206) 463-6157
E-mail: dirk@vashonhostel.com
Website: www.vashonhostel.com

~ what to expect ~

Never spent a night in a covered wagon or a teepee? Never even thought about doing so? Here's your chance to change that.

The 10 acres of forestland on which this family-owned hostel is situated provide a perfect backdrop for the Old West theme its buildings echo. In addition to the teepees and covered wagons, the site includes a log cabin bunkhouse and a two-story refurbished barn. The bunkhouse is home to the men's and women's dorms, one private room and a kitchen. The remodeled barn has a game room, kitchen and TV room. If you elect to sleep in a teepee, you'll find it a bit more sophisticated than those you might have constructed in your backyard as a kid. The floor is concrete, and furnishings include a cot with a thin mattress, a nightstand and an overhead light. The covered wagons aren't too shabby, either, outfitted with double-bed foam mattresses. If you choose either of these options, the hostel will provide a sleeping bag (or two) to make sure you stay warm throughout the night.

If you aren't quite ready for such adventurous sleeping arrangements, you can opt for one of the beds in the dorms or go deluxe and rent the one private room. At the other end of the spectrum, you're welcome to set up your own tent on the adjacent campgrounds.

Free pancake batter is provided each morning, and creative chefs add wild blackberries picked along the island's nature trails. In the evenings, however, many guests choose to ignore the three kitchens available for use and instead toss something on the grill outside.

Teepees and covered wagons are reason enough for most people to explore Vashon. However, road-weary travelers can also use this quiet artists community as a restful base from which to explore Seattle. The hostel provides a daily shuttle to the passenger ferry that will deposit you, after a 15-minute ride, right in the middle of Pike Place Market, Seattle's most popular tourist destination.

~ fast facts ~

Dorm Rates:	$13 HI members, $16 non-members, $11 for groups of 7+ (See Website for teepee and covered wagon rates.)
Season:	May–October
Office Hours:	9am–10pm
Lock-out:	n/a
Size:	80 beds
Private Rooms:	$45–55 for 2
Credit Cards:	MasterCard & Visa
Network:	HI
Beds:	thin, foam mattresses in teepees, covered wagons & dorms; spring mattresses in private room
Kitchen:	yes, 3 separate kitchen facilities
Bathrooms:	house-style
Lockers:	yes, outside
Extras:	free pancake breakfast, pool table, foosball table, basketball court, nature trails, mountain bike rental, kayaking, campfire, gas grill, color TV, videos
Be Aware:	The atmosphere changes significantly when a youth group is present – inquire when making reservations.
In The Area:	horseback riding, beaches, biking
Local Tip:	HI discount on ferries to island; Wolf Town wolf preserve smells terrible – most will want to skip this attraction.
Closest Free Internet:	Vashon public library
Parking:	free parking at hostel; $1.25 shuttle to Seattle ferry

is this hostel great for you?

SOLO WOMEN Yes. Mellow place to relax. Extremely safe.

PARTY ANIMALS Not unless you bring the party with you. No nightlife to speak of.

OVER 30 Yes. Great base camp from which to explore Seattle.

OVER 50 Yes. Bad backs should stick to private room, though.

COUPLES Yes. What could be more romantic than a cozy night spent in a teepee?

FAMILIES Yes. Kids will love this place.

GROUPS Yes. Several big kitchens and indoor common areas.

"Travel makes a wise man better, and a fool worse."

– *Thomas Fuller*

Wisconsin Hostels

1 Madison
HI – Madison

Madison, Wisconsin

HI – MADISON
141 S. Butler St.
Madison, WI 53703
Phone: (608) 441-0144
Fax: (801) 659-4269
E-mail: madisonhostel@yahoo.com
Website: www.madisonhostel.org

~ what to expect ~

Madison has been designated one of the best places to live in the United States.

It has all the hallmarks of a great college town: pedestrian-friendly business district, chummy coffee shops and bookstores and restaurants for sampling every ethnic cuisine.

The hostel itself is next door to a Cuban restaurant. (If you're a java aficionado, you'll soon become addicted to Cuban coffee.)

A few minutes' stroll brings you to the capitol building, and this destination is definitely worth the walk. Evening activities tend to revolve around the restaurants and music venues that are also within walking distance of the hostel.

You'll find this hostel to be friendly and fairly eclectic. The furniture in the common room is typical nondescript hostel décor, but the mural on the wall is something else. Unique and executed in a colorful, stained-glass-window style, it adds interest and vitality to the room it adorns.

Bedrooms are located upstairs. Standard dorms have spring mattresses. Private rooms have metal bunk beds and some have a desk or table and a reading lamp. Free linens are provided for the plastic-covered mattresses in all rooms.

~ fast facts ~

Dorm Rates: $18 HI members
$21 non-members

Private Rooms: $38 HI members
$41 non-members

Credit Cards: MasterCard & Visa

Network: HI

Beds: spring mattresses

Kitchen: yes

Bathrooms: shared, house-style

Lockers: yes

Extras: Internet access, TV, free linens & towels, laundry facilities

Season: all year

Office Hours: 8am–11am & 5pm–9pm

Lock-out: 11am–5pm (winter only)

Size: 29 beds

Be Aware: Hygienic plastic-wrapped mattresses can get noisy under the sheets.

In The Area: state capitol, Main Street shops and restaurants

Local Tip: only a 3-hour drive to/from Chicago

Closest Free Internet: public library

Parking: street parking

is this hostel great for you?

SOLO WOMEN Yes. Laid-back atmosphere.

PARTY ANIMALS Maybe. College town, but not super-happenin'.

OVER 30 Yes. Check out all the great restaurants.

OVER 50 Yes. Convenient location for those on business trips.

COUPLES Yes. Private rooms have double beds.

FAMILIES Maybe, if a small family

GROUPS No. Too small.

Canadian Hostels

1 Vancouver, British Columbia
HI – Vancouver Jericho Beach

2 Victoria, British Columbia
HI – Victoria

Canadian Hostels

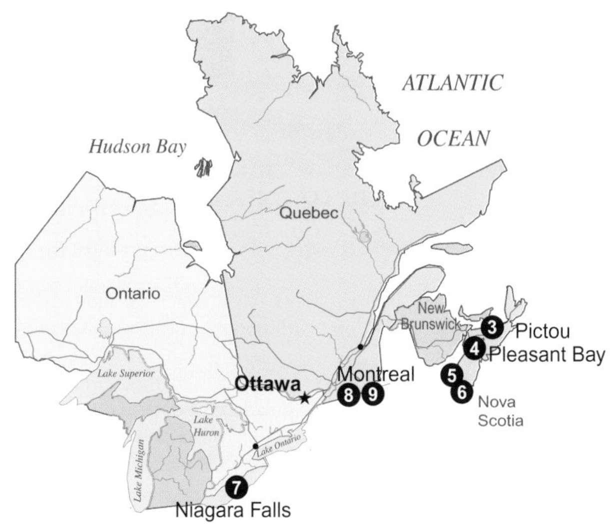

3 Pictou, Nova Scotia
Hostel Pictou

4 Pleasant Bay, Nova Scotia
Cabot Trail Hostel

5 Yarmouth, Nova Scotia
Churchill Mansion B&B and Ice House Hostel

6 Yarmouth, Nova Scotia
Yarmouth Backpackers Accommodation

7 Niagara Falls, Ontario
HI – Niagara Falls

8 Montreal, Quebec
Gite du Parc LaFontaine

9 Montreal, Quebec
Gite du Plateau Mont-Royal

Vancouver, British Columbia

HI – VANCOUVER JERICHO BEACH
1515 Discovery St.
Vancouver, BC V6R 4K5
Phone: (604) 224-3208
Fax: (604) 224-4852
E-mail: van-jericho@hihostels.bc.ca
Website: www.hihostels.bc.ca

~ what to expect ~

This is the best hostel in Vancouver. But I can't recommend it wholeheartedly.

Situated in a park, just one block from the beach, location is what distinguishes this hostel from its competitors. Guests can while away a lazy afternoon with a stroll down to the dock to drink in panoramic views of the city. Or pass the time of day visiting with local fishermen.

However, those wanting more action will discover that getting into the city is no problem. Hostelling International operates a free shuttle between this hostel and its downtown hostels (which aren't as nice as this one). Parking downtown can be pricey and hard to come by. So you may want to exercise this option even if you have a car.

Problems with the bedrooms stand in the way of this hostel receiving an unreserved recommendation. The crowded dorms sleep too many guests in one big room. Although the private rooms alleviate the crowding, a distinct and unpleasant odor permeated mine. Even air freshener supplied by the front desk failed to eliminate the stink. If you decide to stay in a private room here, be sure to check it out before handing over your money.

The onsite café has pros and cons. It can be convenient not to have to make dinner at the end of a long day. But a morning cup of coffee will cost you over $1. And the beer is cheaper here than at the nearby marina restaurant, but the view isn't as good.

The bottom line is that if you're going to be staying in a Vancouver hostel, this is the one to choose. Just lower your expectations a bit before arriving.

~ fast facts ~

Dorm Rates:	$20 CAD HI members $24 CAD non-members
Private Rooms:	$58.50–68.50 CAD
Credit Cards:	MasterCard & Visa
Network:	HI
Beds:	foam mattresses
Kitchen:	yes
Bathrooms:	dorm-style
Lockers:	yes
Extras:	onsite café, pool table, Internet access; free shuttle to downtown HI hostel
Season:	May 1–Sept.1
Office Hours:	24 hours
Lock-out:	n/a
Size:	286 beds
Be Aware:	smelly private rooms, crowded dorms
In The Area:	Gastown cobblestone street shopping district, Granville Island Market, Space Centre, Science World, salmon hatchery, Grouse Mountain Skyride, botanical garden, hiking, kayaking, fishing, skiing within 30 minutes
Local Tip:	$20 CAD 3-course lunch at the Pacific Instituteof Culinary Arts (Granville Island), outdoor Shakespeare festival June–September
Closest Free Internet:	Inquire at desk.
Parking:	inexpensive parking at hostel, free airport/bus station/ train station shuttle

is this hostel great for you?

This hostel needs to make some changes to receive my whole-hearted recommendation. However, it is still a better hostel than the others in town.

Victoria, British Columbia

HI – VICTORIA
516 Yates St.
Victoria, BC V8W 1K8
Phone: (250) 385-4511
Fax: (250) 385-3232
E-mail: Victoria@hihostels.ca
Website: www.hihostels.ca

~ what to expect ~

As Montreal is to France, Victoria is to England.

Stepping off the ferry from Vancouver, you'll feel as though you've just crossed the pond. Cross the street and you can tour the Parliament buildings, round the corner for afternoon tea at the Empress Hotel, hop on a double-decker bus for a city tour and wind up with a visit to the Royal British Columbia Museum. By the end of the day, you'll be humming "God Save the Queen."

This is a fairly large hostel for a fairly small city. The disproportion is appropriate, however, given that tourism is Victoria's main industry. The unfortunate side effect is that guests are crowded into very large dorm rooms. Happily, however, disadvantages typical of other larger hostels are noticeably absent. This hostel is well-maintained: Bedrooms, bathrooms and common areas are all very clean.

Situated on a main street in a safe section of town, this hostel is also conveniently located. Guests can walk to the Inner Harbor to visit tourist attractions, listen to street musicians or relax at an outdoor restaurant and watch the world go by.

This unique, quaint little city makes a perfect side trip to a Vancouver vacation or a good weekend getaway spot all on its own.

~ fast facts ~

Dorm Rates: HI members: $17 – $20

non-members: $21 – $24

Private Rooms: HI members: $39 – $44

non-members: $43 – $48

Credit Cards: MasterCard & Visa

Network: HI

Beds: foam mattresses

Kitchen: yes

Bathrooms: dorm-style

Lockers: yes

Extras: pool table, video games, TV, library, laundry, Internet access

Be Aware: crowded dorms

In The Area: afternoon tea, whale watching, botanical gardens, Royal British Columbia Museum, Miniature World, Maritime Museum

Local Tip: May–September is best for spotting whales.

Closest Free Internet: library

Parking: free evening street parking, $5/day lot parking

Season: all year

Office Hours: 24 hours

Lock-out: n/a

Size: 110 beds

is this hostel great for you?

SOLO WOMEN Yes. Too big to be cozy, but safe, comfortable and with plenty to do.

PARTY ANIMALS Yes. The hostel isn't raucous, but plenty of pubs are nearby.

OVER 30 Yes. Relax in the sunny upstairs common room.

OVER 50 Yes. Many mature travelers enjoy the elegant afternoon tea experience.

COUPLES Yes.

FAMILIES Not especially.

GROUPS Yes. Large dining and common rooms are available.

Pictou, Nova Scotia

HOSTEL PICTOU
14 Chapel
Box 1792
Pictou, NS B0K 1H0
Phone: (902) 485-8740
Fax: n/a
E-mail: hostelpictou@hotmail.com
Website: www.backpackers.ca

~ what to expect ~

Pictou is the quintessential Nova Scotia town. With a historic downtown, a harbor, a ferry to the islands and a summer lobster festival, it has everything that makes Nova Scotia special. And this civilized little hostel is within walking distance of it all.

The entire hostel sleeps just nine guests, but those guests get a lot of personal attention. The owners enjoy hosting visitors and introducing them to their town. The wife even leads free walking tours of Pictou every Sunday.

The owners' little white house encompasses the hostel. The kitchen on the main floor is equipped with a table that seats six and all the pots, pans and dishes required to prepare and serve a meal. There's a big-screen TV in the den next door.

Each of the three pastel upstairs bedrooms has its own theme and contains pictures of, and information about, the local historical figure the décor reflects. Guests sleep in twin beds, either two or three in a room, and there's no charge for sheets and bedspreads. The rooms operate as either dorms or private rooms, depending on guests' preference. Upon arrival, guests may notice a candle, a novel or some other personal touch. A stay at this hostel will feel like quite an upgrade for those used to sterile, metal-bunk-bedded dorms.

The weather dictates that this seasonal hostel is open only during the summer and fall. But whenever you arrive, the town and the hostel will welcome you.

~ fast facts ~

Dorm Rates: $20 CAD

Private Rooms: $40 CAD

Credit Cards: n/a

Network: Backpackers

Season: May–September

Office Hours: 5pm–9pm

Lock-out: n/a

Size: 9 beds

Beds: spring mattresses

Kitchen: yes

Bathrooms: shared

Lockers: yes–2

Extras: free sheets

Be Aware: The owner has pet cats.

In The Area: historic harbor

Local Tip: July lobster festival, August "Hector" festival

Closest Free Internet: public library, 2 blocks away

Parking: Free onsite parking, pick-up service from bus in New Glasgow or ferry in Caribou can be arranged.

is this hostel great for you?

SOLO WOMEN Yes. Owners live on second floor, for added security.

PARTY ANIMALS No. Too quiet.

OVER 30 Yes. Take advantage of the free Sunday walking tour.

OVER 50 Yes. You'll enjoy the friendly owners.

COUPLES Maybe. Cozy atmosphere, but no double beds.

FAMILIES No. No family rooms available.

GROUPS No. Too small.

Pleasant Bay, Nova Scotia

CABOT TRAIL HOSTEL
23349 Cabot Trail
Pleasant Bay, NS B9E 2P0
Phone: (902) 224-1976
Fax: n/a
E-mail: hostel@cabottrail.com
Website: www.cabottrail.com

~ what to expect ~

With two basic coed dorm rooms and a coed 10-person bunkhouse, this hostel is best appreciated by hikers used to "roughing it." Each of the dorms has two sets of bunk beds; the rooms have neither lockers nor doors. Common areas include a kitchen and a small TV room.

While the accommodations are pretty rustic, the management is very friendly and makes every effort to accommodate any hosteller who shows up needing a place to stay.

The hostel is set in the middle of the Cape Breton Highlands National Park, about half-way 'round the scenic Cape Breton drive. It's a beautiful drive and an even better hike.

~ fast facts ~

Dorm Rates: $20 CAD

Private Rooms: n/a

Credit Cards: MasterCard & Visa

Network: n/a

Beds: spring mattresses

Kitchen: yes

Bathrooms: shared, dorm-style

Lockers: no

Extras: donation Internet access, free linens, barbecue, pay phone

Be Aware: pretty rustic

In The Area: Cabot Trail scenic drive, hiking, whale watching, sea kayaking

Local Tip: Ask about lobster/crab boil.

Closest Free Internet: community Internet facility

Parking: free onsite parking

Season: May – Nov.

Office Hours: 24 hours

Lock-out: no

Size: 20 beds

is this hostel great for you?

SOLO WOMEN Maybe. Only if into hiking and OK with coed dorms.

PARTY ANIMALS No. Quiet area.

OVER 30 Maybe. See "solo women."

OVER 50 No. Serious lack of privacy.

COUPLES No. No private rooms.

FAMILIES No. Too small.

GROUPS Yes, if rent 10-person bunkhouse.

Yarmouth, Nova Scotia

CHURCHILL MANSION B&B
& ICE HOUSE HOSTEL

RR #1
Yarmouth, NS B5A 4A5
Phone: (902) 649-2818
Fax: (902) 649-2801
E-mail: churchillmansion@auracom.com
Website: n/a

~ what to expect ~

The Churchill Mansion B&B was built in the 1890s as the summer home of a wealthy man. Many of the original light fixtures, woodwork and floor coverings of this registered historic property are still in place.

The Mansion reopened as a country inn in 1981 and now serves as a popular destination for family reunions, retreats, workshops and weddings. Guests enjoy swimming or canoeing on the lake or antiquing in town.

Hostel accommodations attached to the B&B consist of three private rooms and two coed dorm rooms. Each of the private rooms is furnished with one double bed. Two of these rooms share a bath; the third has a private, handicapped-accessible bath. The twin-bedded dorms share a bathroom.

The hostellers' common room fosters low-key relaxation. But hostel guests also have access to the common rooms in The Mansion. The antique-filled sitting room may be a little too fancy for all but the most sophisticated of hostellers, but everyone will appreciate the dining room. Amazing lake views are on the house, and three meals a day and an occasional seafood buffet can be had for an additional charge.

This is a hostel for grown-ups. It's one of the few that caters to older, more discriminating travelers.

~ fast facts ~

Dorm Rates: $14 CAD

Private Rooms: same as dorms

Credit Cards: MasterCard & Visa

Network: n/a

Beds: thin foam mattresses with plastic covers in dorm, spring mattresses in private rooms

Kitchen: yes

Bathrooms: shared, house-style

Lockers: no

Extras: free canoe usage, meals available for purchase, gift shop, Internet access

Be Aware: 10 miles outside of town

In The Area: fishing villages, antique shops, county museum, parks, beaches, Darling Lake

Local Tip: medieval festival held onsite in June

Closest Free Internet: unknown

Parking: free onsite parking, free shuttle to ferry

Season: year-round

Office Hours: 24 hours

Lock-out: n/a

Size: 12 beds

is this hostel great for you?

SOLO WOMEN Yes. Relaxed, country inn environment.

PARTY ANIMALS No. Would bore you to death.

OVER 30 Yes. Nice private rooms.

OVER 50 Yes. Great hostel for older travelers.

COUPLES Yes. Very romantic atmosphere.

FAMILIES Yes, if renting four-person dorm room.

GROUPS Maybe. Small groups can rent the entire hostel.

Yarmouth, Nova Scotia

YARMOUTH BACKPACKERS ACCOMMODATION
6 Trinity Place
Yarmouth, NS B5A 1P4
Phone: (902) 749-0941
Fax: n/a
E-mail: yarmouthbackpackers@hotmail.com
Website: www.yarmouthbackpackers.com

~ what to expect ~

Downtown Yarmouth now has a hostel, thanks to a young couple who decided to renovate the top floor of their house to accommodate travelers. Those disembarking from the U.S. ferry are forever indebted to them.

A separate entrance provides access to the hostel section of the house. After climbing stairs, guests will find that although common areas are minimal, the hostel accommodations are quite nice.

There is no hostel kitchen or dining room per se, but guests are welcome to use the owners' kitchen and take meals to the little hostel sitting room.

Bedrooms include two private rooms and one coed dorm. One private room is furnished with a double bed; the other has two twin beds. The dorm has four twin beds, and all three rooms share two brand-new bathrooms. Drapes accent windows throughout the hostel and throw rugs add splashes of color to hardwood floors.

Best known as the Canadian port for the ferry that runs to and from the United States, Yarmouth isn't an especially exciting town. However, the beaches, spectacular sunsets and local seafood can make low-maintenance guests happy campers for a couple of days.

~ fast facts ~

Dorm Rates: $20 CAD

Private Rooms: $46 CAD

Credit Cards: no

Network: Backpackers Hostel Canada

Beds: mixed in dorms, spring mattresses in private

Kitchen: yes

Bathrooms: shared, dorm-style

Lockers: no

Extras: TV, Internet access, bike storage

Season: May–October (other dates by arrangement)

Office Hours: 8am–10pm

Lock-out: no

Size: 8 beds

Be Aware: Yarmouth isn't really an exciting town.

In The Area: museums, beaches, lakes, cycling, tours

Local Tip: Private shuttles to/from Halifax are more convenient than the bus line.

Closest Free Internet: unknown

Parking: street parking; walking distance of U.S. ferry terminal

is this hostel great for you?

SOLO WOMEN Yes. Choose a private room, though, if you aren't up for a coed dorm.

PARTY ANIMALS Not especially.

OVER 30 Yes. Good hostel value.

OVER 50 Yes, so long as stairs aren't an issue.

COUPLES Yes. One private room has a double bed.

FAMILIES Maybe. Families of four can rent the dorm.

GROUPS No. Too small.

Niagara Falls, Ontario

HI – NIAGARA FALLS
4549 Cataract Ave.
Niagara Falls, ON L2E 3M2
Phone: (888) 749-0058
Fax: (905) 357-7673
E-mail: Niagara.falls@hihostels.ca
Website: www.hihostels.ca

~ what to expect ~

Visitors to Niagara Falls can choose to stay on the Canadian side of the Falls or on the American side. It's an easy choice to make. The Canadian side has more to see and do. And it has the better hostel.

A plain, rectangular brick building with no adornment except the HI sign, the hostel looks pretty unimpressive from the outside. But that first impression makes the interior a pleasant surprise.

Color and personality abound inside. The furniture in the basement-level common room may be ugly, but the red walls and blue ceiling create an atmosphere that's downright festive. And the whole place is warmed by a wood-burning stove.

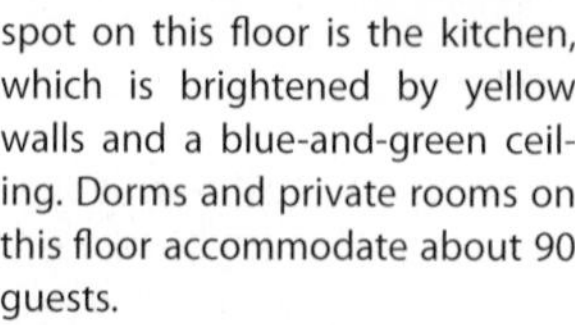

The rooms upstairs are just as much fun. The primary gathering spot on this floor is the kitchen, which is brightened by yellow walls and a blue-and-green ceiling. Dorms and private rooms on this floor accommodate about 90 guests.

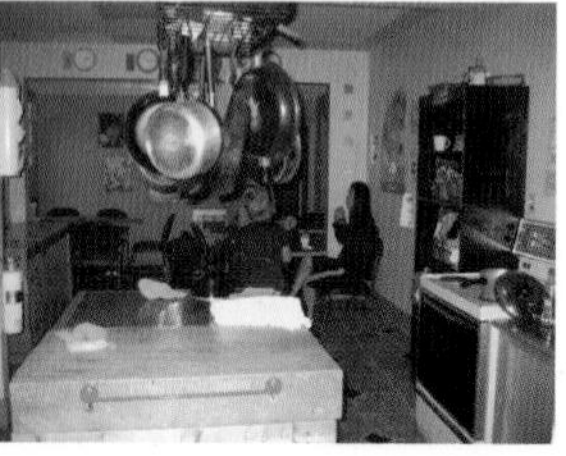

Most people come to town to see the giant waterfalls – and for good reason. The second-largest falls on the planet are pretty amazing from any angle. Some spots in town offer premium views of the top of these natural wonders. And if you have money to spend on one attraction, spring for a Maid of the Mist cruise to the base of the Falls. It's an experience you won't soon forget.

~ fast facts ~

Dorm Rates: $19 CAD–HI members
$23 CAD non-members

Private Rooms: $50 CAD–HI members
$42 CAD non-members

Credit Cards: MasterCard, Visa & JCB

Network: HI

Beds: foam mattresses

Kitchen: yes

Bathrooms: shared, house-style

Lockers: yes, big ones in basement ($2 CAD)

Extras: Internet access, TV, videos, laundry facilities

Season: all year

Office Hours: 24 hours (summer) 8am–10pm (winter)

Lock-out: n/a

Size: 88 beds

Be Aware: some dorms coed (not all)

In The Area: Niagara Falls waterfalls, tourist shops

Local Tip: This hostel is better than the one on the U.S. side of Niagara Falls.

Closest Free Internet: public library

Parking: free onsite parking,1½ blocks from bus station and VIA train station

is this hostel great for you?

SOLO WOMEN Yes. Friendly place.

PARTY ANIMALS Maybe. No alcohol allowed in hostel, but lots of bars in town.

OVER 30 Yes. Lots to do in town

OVER 50 Yes. Private rooms available.

COUPLES Yes. Niagara Falls is famous as a romantic destination.

FAMILIES Yes. Kids will enjoy the tacky tourist attractions in town.

GROUPS Not especially.

Montreal, Quebec

GITE DU PARC LAFONTAINE
1250 Sherbrooke E.
Montreal, QC H2L 1M1
Phone: (877) 350-4483 or (514) 522-3910
Fax: (514) 844-7356
E-mail: info@hostelmontreal.com
Website: www.hostelmontreal.com

~ what to expect ~

Smaller sister to the Gite du Plateau Mont-Royal, this hostel is an excellent choice for those in town during the summer months.

This hostel has a smaller living room and smaller dorms than its sister. And it doesn't have a dining room. But other amenities set it apart.

A free continental breakfast is served on the covered outdoor deck each morning. Guests who want to cook for themselves are welcome to use the kitchen. Pastel walls, flowing curtains and coordinated spreads give the private bedrooms a decorator's touch. Fresh flowers enhance the bistro atmosphere; one room even has a little balcony. Rooms have either one double bed, a set of bunks or a combination of both.

If you don't require a private room, you can opt for a coed or segregated dorm. The coed dorm sleeps up to eight people. Each of the smaller segregated dorms holds only four beds. Be forewarned, though: The private rooms are tidy, but the dorms can get pretty messy.

The hostel is in a good neighborhood and stays in the neighbors' good graces by locking the doors at 11pm. Each guest is given a key to the front door, but is asked to be quiet when returning to the hostel.

Whichever of the two recommended hostels you choose in Montreal, you won't go wrong.

~ fast facts ~

Dorm Rates:	$24 CAD ISIC members $25 CAD non-members	**Season:**	June–August
Private Rooms:	$55–75 CAD (1 or 2 people)	**Office Hours:**	8am–11pm
Credit Cards:	no	**Lock-out:**	no
Network:	n/a	**Size:**	28 beds

Beds: spring & foam mattresses (covered in plastic)

Kitchen: yes

Bathrooms: shared

Lockers: yes

Extras: free breakfast, free linens, laundry, luggage storage, Internet access

Be Aware: closed most of the year

In The Area: Montreal sights

Local Tip: The owner of this hostel also owns Gite du Plateau Mont-Royal. Both are equally good choices.

Closest Free Internet: unknown

Parking: street parking; close to Sherbrooke Metro stop

is this hostel great for you?

SOLO WOMEN Yes. Very pretty hostel.

PARTY ANIMALS Maybe, if quiet after 11pm.

OVER 30 Yes.

OVER 50 Yes, but only if staying in a private room.

COUPLES Yes. Double beds available in private rooms and coed dorms.

FAMILIES Yes, if no more than four in family.

GROUPS No. Too small.

Montreal, Quebec

GITE DU PLATEAU MONT-ROYAL
185 Sherbrooke E.
Montreal, QC H2X 1C7
Phone: (877) 350-4483 or (514) 284-1276
Fax: (514) 844-7356
E-mail: info@hostelmontreal.com
Website: www.hostelmontreal.com

~ what to expect ~

Bright and inviting, this hostel is the best year-round choice for visitors to Montreal. The owners have a second hostel that is equally good, but it's open only during the summer.

Set amongst lovely brownstones, the hostel is in a good, safe neighborhood. Hardwood floors and abundant windows impart the aura of a sophisticated café or coffeehouse.

Dorms are upstairs in this three-story hostel. Common rooms are on the first floor, and private rooms are in the basement. Common rooms include a kitchen, dining room and living room. The kitchen is limited and open only during dinner hours. Guests needn't worry about their morning meal, though: A free breakfast is provided in the dining room each day.

The dorms are furnished with dressers, mirrors, chairs and bunk beds. Sinks and oscillating fans provide added comfort. Free towels are provided in private rooms furnished with one double bed, one set of bunk beds or two twin beds. Cleanliness is taken seriously here. A cleaning staff makes sure the linens are laundered and the rooms are tidy.

This hostel is safe, clean, well-located and full of atmosphere. On all counts, it's the best hostel in town.

~ fast facts ~

Dorm Rates:	$25 CAD	**Season:**	year-round
Private Rooms:	$55+ CAD	**Office Hours:**	8am–11pm
Credit Cards:	no	**Lock-out:**	n/a
Network:	n/a	**Size:**	42 beds

Beds: mix of foam and spring mattresses

Kitchen: yes

Bathrooms: shared

Lockers: yes

Extras: free breakfast, free linens

Be Aware: Reservations are advised during festivals.

In The Area: Montreal sights

Local Tip: onsite Internet café ($1 CAN/15 minutes)

Closest Free Internet: unknown

Parking: street parking; near Sherbrooke Metro station

is this hostel great for you?

SOLO WOMEN Yes. Nicest hostel in town.

PARTY ANIMALS Yes. No curfew any more.

OVER 30 Yes. Grown-up clientele.

OVER 50 Yes. Good private rooms.

COUPLES Yes. Double beds available in the private rooms.

FAMILIES Yes. Large private room sleeps up to eight people.

GROUPS Not especially.

Index